N

TWO PLAYS

Marivaux

TWO PLAYS

THE TRIUMPH OF LOVE

Translated and adapted by
Braham Murray and Katherine Sand

THE GAME OF LOVE AND CHANCE

Translated and adapted by Neil Bartlett

OBERON BOOKS
LONDON

First published in 2007 by Oberon Books Ltd
521 Caledonian Road, London N7 9RH
Tel: 020 7607 3637 / Fax: 020 7607 3629
e-mail: info@oberonbooks.com
www.oberonbooks.com

Contents

THE TRIUMPH OF LOVE

Translated and adapted
by Braham Murray and Katherine Sand

Characters

LEONIDA
Princess of Sparta, under the name of PHOCION

CORINA
Servant to Leonida under the name of HERMIDAS

HERMOCRATES
Philosopher

LEONTINA
Sister of Hermocrates

AGIS
Son of Cleomene

DIMAS
Hermocrates' gardener

HARLEQUIN
Hermocrates' valet

The play takes place in Hermocrates' garden.

This translation of *The Triumph of Love* was first produced at the Royal Exchange Theatre, Manchester, on 17 April 2007, with the following cast:

LEONIDA (PHOCION), Rae Hendrie

CORINA (HERMIDAS), Sarah Paul

HERMOCRATES, Terence Wilton

LEONTINA, Brigit Forsyth

AGIS, Charlie Anson

DIMAS, John Axon

HARLEQUIN, Michael Moreland

Director Braham Murray

Designer Simon Higlett

Lighting Johanna Town

Sound Steve Brown

Company Manager Nick Chesterfield

Stage Manager Francis Lynch

Deputy Stage Manager Tracey Fleet

Assistant Stage Manager Lizzie Frankl

Act One

(*LEONIDA under the name PHOCION. CORINA under the name HERMIDAS.*)

PHOCION: We are here! The gardens of Hermocrates the philosopher.

HERMIDAS: But, madam, we don't know anyone here. Won't they mind us just walking in like this?

PHOCION: Why? They've left it unlocked and we've simply come to speak to the master of the house. Let us continue on this path and I will explain everything you need to know as we go along.

HERMIDAS: This is a delightful place. I have not felt so at ease for a long time. But if it's not too much to ask maybe the Princess will indulge my fevered imagination and allow me to ask some questions about what on earth is going on.

PHOCION: Whatever you like.

HERMIDAS: You leave the court and the town and you travel here to one of your country residences accompanied by only a handful of your servants and you ask me to follow you.

PHOCION: Quite right.

HERMIDAS: One morning after we have been here four or five days, you take me to a room, you lock the doors, you show me two portraits and ask me to make miniature copies of them. One is a man about forty-five years old, the other a woman about thirty-five, both quite good looking.

PHOCION: True.

HERMIDAS: Let me go on. When I have finished the copies you let it be known that you are unwell and that no one may see you. Next you dress me as a man, you get yourself up the same way and we set off together incognito in this carriage. You call yourself Phocion and give me the name Hermidas and after travelling for a quarter of an hour we arrive here in the gardens of the philosopher Hermocrates – but I don't believe you are here to discuss philosophy with him.

PHOCION: It's more likely than you might think.

11

HERMIDAS: What do the faked illness and the copied portraits mean? Who are the man and woman? Why are we dressed up? What are we doing in Hermocrates' garden? What do you want of him? What do you want of me? Where are we going? What will happen to us? Where is it all leading to? Tell me before I burst.

PHOCION: Listen carefully. You know how I came to rule this land. Cleomenes was the prince. My Uncle Leonidas commanded the army. Cleomenes fell in love with my uncle's wife. My uncle was away fighting a war for Cleomenes. Cleomenes abducted my aunt. The army sided with my uncle. My uncle seized the kingdom and captured them both. They died within six months. On her deathbed my aunt gave birth to a little prince. Someone stole him from the Court. My uncle searched high and low but never found him. My uncle died, his brother, my father succeeded him. My father died. Here I am.

HERMIDAS: That doesn't answer my questions! Why are we disguised? What are the portraits I have copied? Tell me!

PHOCION: Calm down! I know where the little prince is!

HERMIDAS: Excellent! You will soon have him in your power.

PHOCION: Not at all. It is I who will be in his power.

HERMIDAS: You most certainly will not be! I will not allow it!

PHOCION: Allow me to finish. This prince has lived with Hermocrates the philosopher, a man of great austerity and wisdom, since he was eight years old. I know this from a servant who has been in Hermocrates' service and who informed on him to me hoping to gain some reward.

HERMIDAS: That is of no importance, you must protect your position, madam.

PHOCION: I intend the opposite. I have decided to be fair, I don't know what possessed me to think of being anything else. First of all I wanted to see Agis (that is the Prince's name). I learned that he and Hermocrates walked in the forest next to my chateau every day. So I left the town as you know and came here, without my retinue. It was then that I saw Agis for the first time. The servant who was waiting for me showed me the Prince reading deep in the forest. I had heard about love but it was just a word to me. Imagine, Corina, all the Graces. Take their most beautiful and noble features. Put them together in one being and you will still fall short of Agis.

HERMIDAS: Could this be what's so attractive about the countryside all of a sudden?

PHOCION: Let me finish. Just as I was leaving Hermocrates appeared and asked me whether the Princess ever walked in the forest, so it was clear that he did not recognise me. I was flustered but I told him that she did indeed stay nearby and I returned to the chateau.

HERMIDAS: That's an adventure.

PHOCION: There's more to come. I pretended to be ill and refused to see anyone so I could be free to come here. As far as Hermocrates is concerned I am Phocion, a young traveller, who has heard of his great wisdom and begs to spend some time here to study at his feet. In this guise I'll work on Agis' heart. He hates my family so he mustn't know who I am until I've won him over completely.

HERMIDAS: Yes, madam, but what if Hermocrates recognises you in your man's clothes as the lady he spoke to in the forest? He wouldn't let you stay.

PHOCION: I've thought of that, Corina. If he recognises me it will be the worse for him. I have set a trap which all his wisdom will not save him from. I don't want to use it but my mission has a higher calling – I am inspired by love and justice. I just need two or three conversations with Agis. I must have them. There is no other way.

HERMIDAS: What about his sister? If she's as austere as him, will she consent to a stranger as young and handsome as you staying here?

PHOCION: If she gets in my way I will show her no more mercy than I would to her brother.

HERMIDAS: But, madam, if I understand you correctly you will be tricking both of them. Isn't that shocking?

PHOCION: It would be if my cause was not just. Hermocrates and his sister will deserve their punishment. They don't know anything about me, they don't know the goodness of my soul. But that has not stopped them from poisoning Agis against me for years. The servant I bribed told me this. Even worse, they have raised armies against me that I have had to fight and they continue to plot. But I am innocent. I did not usurp the throne and I didn't know till now that the legitimate heir is alive. I have wronged no one so I have no compunction about what I am going to do. No, Corina, my conscience is clear. Most important of all take good care of the copies of the portraits you have made – they are of Hermocrates and his sister – I may need them. Make sure you know everything that happens and I will tell you what needs to be done.

(*Enter HARLEQUIN, a valet, not seen at first.*)

HARLEQUIN: (*Aside.*) Who are these people?

HERMIDAS: This won't be easy, madam, and your sex…

HARLEQUIN: (*Surprising them.*) Aha! Madam! What about your sex? Eh! Speak gentlemen, or are you in fact ladies?

PHOCION: Oh my god!

HARLEQUIN: Just a minute little ladies. Don't run off I want to know who you are. I took you for two knaves. My apologies. You're a pair of queens!

PHOCION: Corina! We've lost before we've begun.

HERMIDAS: (*Signalling to PHOCION.*) No, madam, let me take care of this and don't be afraid. Look at this boy. I am certain that we can manage.

HARLEQUIN: And not only that but I'm an honest man who doesn't deal in smuggled goods. So I am shutting the gates.

HERMIDAS: Don't do that. You'll be sorry for the wrong you are doing.

HARLEQUIN: Show me how sorry I'd be and I'll let you go.

PHOCION: (*Giving several pieces of gold to HARLEQUIN.*) Here, this is the proof. Wouldn't you have been sorry to have missed that?

HARLEQUIN: Well I'm certainly happy enough to have it.

HERMIDAS: Do you still want to make a fuss?

HARLEQUIN: I'm beginning not to want to.

HERMIDAS: Help him make his mind up, madam.

PHOCION: (*Giving him more.*) Better?

HARLEQUIN: Amazing! All of a sudden my bad mood is disappearing. So tell me honestly most generous ladies, what is this all about?

HERMIDAS: Look, it is nothing really. Madam saw Agis in the forest and she fell in love with him.

HARLEQUIN: That's honest!

HERMIDAS: Madam is rich and since she wants to marry him, she wants him to know about it.

HARLEQUIN: Very honest!

HERMIDAS: The only way Madam can think of doing this is to stay in the house where he lives and engage him in conversation.

HARLEQUIN: It's a very nice house.

HERMIDAS: And that could not happen if she introduced herself dressed as her own sex. Firstly because Hermocrates would not allow it and secondly because Agis would run away from her because of what he has been taught by the philosopher.

HARLEQUIN: Good god! Love in this house? This is no home for love. Pool the wisdom of Agis, Hermocrates and Leontina and you'll find such a great weight of learning that makes this the worst place for love in the world. There's only me here with any kind of idea about that can of worms.

PHOCION: So we see.

HERMIDAS: And this is why Madam has taken the trouble to disguise herself. So you see there is nothing at all wrong.

HARLEQUIN: What could be more reasonable! Madam has by chance fallen in love with Agis. So what? It seems to me that you should take what you can get. Go, gracious ladies, good luck and I offer you my services. You have lost your heart so do all you can to trap another. Incidentally if anyone wants mine they can have it.

PHOCION: You can go now. I assure you, soon you won't need to envy anyone else.

HERMIDAS: Do not forget that Madam's name is Phocion and I am Hermidas.

PHOCION: And Agis must not know who we are.

HARLEQUIN: Have no fear my dear Phocion, shake on it brother Hermidas. You like the way I'm talking?

HERMIDAS: Quiet, someone's coming.

(*Enter DIMAS, a gardener.*)

DIMAS: Who are you talking to, flower?

HARLEQUIN: Eh? Just people.

DIMAS: I can see that but who are these people and what do they want?

PHOCION: Lord Hermocrates.

DIMAS: Well this isn't the way you come in. Our master has ordered me to stop people walking around the garden. So turn round, go back where you came from and knock on the gate of the lodge.

PHOCION: We found the garden gate open. Strangers are allowed to lose their way.

DIMAS: I don't allow them. People can't come in here just like that. You think an open gate is an invitation to walk through. You should have the decency to call a gardener, ask him for the privilege. If you show good manners, then the gate will be opened to you.

HARLEQUIN: Gently my friend, you are speaking to a rich and important person.

DIMAS: I can see he is rich because he behaves like he owns everything. Well I look after my garden, he has to go round the other way.

(*Enter AGIS.*)

AGIS: What is all this noise about, gardener? Why are you shouting?

DIMAS: This young man has come to steal our trees.

PHOCION: Sir, you have arrived just in time. My only wish is to greet Lord Hermocrates and to speak to him. I found this gate open and now he wants me to leave by it.

AGIS: Dimas, you are mistaken, leave us and warn Leontina that a stranger of importance wishes to speak to Hermocrates, quickly. (*Exit DIMAS.*) Sir I beg your pardon for this man's rustic welcome. Hermocrates will apologise to you himself. I can see from your face the respect that we owe you.

HARLEQUIN: Yes, they're a pretty pair.

PHOCION: It is true, sir, that the gardener treated me roughly but your kindness has made up for that. If my face disposes you to think well of me, I should believe it to be the happiest face alive. It could not have done me a greater service.

AGIS: You should not praise it for that, it is no great prize. However, it has had that effect. Although we have only known each other a few moments, no one could be as well disposed towards a person as I am to you.

HARLEQUIN: (*Aside.*) We're going to make a very happy quartet.

HERMIDAS: (*Takes HARLEQUIN aside.*) Let's go for a walk. We've got a lot to talk about.

AGIS: May I ask to whom I have declared my friendship?

PHOCION: To someone who would willingly swear his to you for an eternity.

AGIS: You must tell me more. I am afraid to make a friend that I might soon lose.

PHOCION: If it were up to me I would not wish us ever to leave each other.

AGIS: What do you want of Hermocrates? I owe him my education and I am so bold as to say that he loves me. Do you have some need of him?

PHOCION: I was drawn here by his reputation. When I arrived here all I wanted was to try and spend some time in his company. But since knowing you, that plan has been overtaken by something even more urgent, which is to spend as much time as I can with you.

AGIS: And what will become of you after that?

PHOCION: I do not know, you will decide. You alone.

AGIS: I would advise you never to leave my sight.

PHOCION: Then we shall be together for ever.

AGIS: I hope so with all my heart. But here comes Leontina.

HARLEQUIN: (*To HERMIDAS.*) Our mistress is here: I don't like that look on her face.

(*Enter DIMAS and LEONTINA.*)

DIMAS: Madam, this is the man I told you about, and this little
bumblebee is his sidekick.

LEONTINA: Sir, I am told that you wish to speak to
Hermocrates my brother. He is not here at present. Could
you tell me what you have to say to him?

PHOCION: I have nothing secret to tell him, madam. It
concerns a favour I wish to obtain from him. I believe I
could obtain it now if you granted it to me yourself.

LEONTINA: Explain yourself, sir.

PHOCION: I am called Phocion, madam: my name may be
known to you. It was well known through my father who
died some years ago.

LEONTINA: Yes of course, sir.

PHOCION: In my loneliness I have been travelling for some
time to feed my heart and spirit.

DIMAS: (*Aside.*) With the fruit from our trees.

LEONTINA: Leave us Dimas. (*Exit DIMAS.*)

PHOCION: During my travels I have visited those whose
knowledge and virtue distinguish them from other men.
Many of them have allowed me to stay a while with them
and I hoped that the widely famed Hermocrates would not
refuse me the honour of just a few days in that same spirit.

LEONTINA: Your appearance suggests that you are worthy
of the hospitality that you received elsewhere. But it will
not be possible for Hermocrates to do himself the honour
of offering you the same. Important reasons which, Agis
knows well, prevent us. If I could tell you them you would
understand.

HARLEQUIN: I'll put one of them up in my room.

AGIS: We are not short of rooms.

LEONTINA: No. You know better than anyone Agis that this
cannot be. We have made it a rule not to share our retreat
with anyone.

AGIS: But I promised Phocion that I would persuade you.
Surely it would not break our rule to make an exception
for a virtuous friend?

LEONTINA: I cannot change my mind.

HARLEQUIN: (*Aside.*) Women!

PHOCION: Why are you so inflexible, madam, when my intentions are so honourable?

LEONTINA: It is despite myself.

AGIS: Hermocrates will sway you, madam.

LEONTINA: I am certain that he will share my views.

PHOCION: (*First words aside.*) I'll have to think fast. Well, madam, I will insist no further but may I dare to ask for a private word with you?

LEONTINA: I am tired of your pleas but since you wish it I consent.

PHOCION: (*To AGIS.*) Please be so good as to leave us alone for a moment.

(*Exit AGIS, HERMIDAS, HARLEQUIN.*)

PHOCION: (*First words spoken aside.*) For love's sake let me lie brilliantly! Madam, since you cannot consent to my request I shall not press you but perhaps you will do me a different favour. I need some advice from you that will determine the course of the whole of the rest of my life.

LEONTINA: The only advice I will give you is to wait for Hermocrates, he can advise you better than I.

PHOCION: No, madam, on this occasion you will be better than him. I need someone with a more compassionate mind. I need a heart which tempers its severity with softness and that sweet mixture is found more often in your sex than in ours. So, madam, by all that is good in you, hear me, I beg you.

LEONTINA: I do not know what you mean but you have an air of distinction so I shall listen to you.

PHOCION: Some days ago on my travels I saw a woman walking near here. She did not see me. I shall describe her for you. Perhaps you will recognise her and then you will understand better what I am talking about. She was not tall but she was regal; I have never seen so noble an air. She had a unique face; tenderness, nobility, modesty and, yes, austerity shone together from her. She had to be loved but cautiously because she was awe-inspiring. She was young, not that white-hot youth which attracts the eyes but does not melt the heart. No, she was of that age most worthy of love where all the graces join forces, when the whole being is united, that age when beauty is enhanced with the finest gold, mined from the depths of the soul.

LEONTINA: (*Embarrassed.*) No, I do not recognise her, this lady is not known to me. I am sure you are overpraising her.

PHOCION: The portrait I keep in my heart is a thousand times more beautiful than the one I am painting you, madam. I told you that I was only passing through here on my travels, but this creature stopped me and I could not let her out of my sight as long as it was still possible to see her. The lady was speaking to someone, she smiled from time to time and I discerned in her a kind of softness, generosity and kindliness which infused her serious and modest manner.

LEONTINA: (*Aside.*) Who is he talking about?

PHOCION: She withdrew soon afterwards and returned to a nearby house. I asked who she was and I learned that she is the sister of a celebrated and respected man.

LEONTINA: (*Aside.*) What is happening?

PHOCION: I found out that she is not married and that she lives with this brother in seclusion. She prefers the peace of innocence to the tumult of a world hostile to virtuous and sublime souls. Indeed all that I learned of her was praiseworthy and my mind as much as my heart determined that I would give myself to her for ever.

LEONTINA: (*Moved.*) Sir, spare me the rest, I do not know what love is and I would advise you badly about something I do not understand.

PHOCION: I beg you, let me finish and do not let the word 'love' repel you. The love I speak to you about does not soil my heart, it honours it. It is my love of virtue that lights up the love I have for this lady. These two loves unite in me and if I do love her, if I do adore that lovely face it is because my soul sees in it the image of its own beauty.

LEONTINA: Once more, sir, allow me to leave you, I am expected elsewhere. We have spent enough time together.

PHOCION: I have nearly finished, madam. I was overwhelmed by the feelings I have spoken of. With joy in my heart I promised to love her all my life. I promised to devote my days to the service of virtue itself. I resolved to speak to her brother and under the pretext of learning from him try to obtain the happiness of spending time at his house and there, to surround her with love, respect and devotion. To submit to her, to work for her, to prove to her a passion so true that it can only have come from the gods.

LEONTINA: (*Aside.*) How can I get out of this?

PHOCION: I did what I had decided to do. I came to speak to her brother. He wasn't there and I found her alone. I tried to press my case, she rejected it and I was thrown into despair. Imagine, madam, my trembling and frustrated heart. She must have noticed its tenderness and pain. It should have softened her if only to pity me. But I was denied, madam, and in this appalling situation I turn to you. (*He falls to his knees.*)

LEONTINA: What are you doing, sir?

PHOCION: I beg for your advice and your help with her.

LEONTINA: The gods should give me some advice for myself.

PHOCION: The advice of the gods is already in your heart. Believe what it says.

LEONTINA: In my heart? You want me to consult the enemy of my peace?

PHOCION: And will you be less peaceful if you are merciful?

LEONTINA: Ah Phocion, you say you love virtue but love has caught it off guard.

PHOCION: Is that all you can call this adoration?

LEONTINA: But what will you do?

PHOCION: I have devoted my life to you, I want to unite it with yours. Do not stop me from trying, allow me to spend just a few days here. It is the only favour I desire and if you grant it to me, I know Hermocrates will agree.

LEONTINA: Allow you to stay when you say you love me?

PHOCION: My love will make me respect you more.

LEONTINA: If your love was virtuous it would not try to corrupt another. Do you want my heart to lose its way? What have you come here to do Phocion? What is happening? Must my mind be overthrown? Is this possible? This is uncharted territory. I have never loved; must I love you? Must I become vulnerable? No, your flattery is in vain; you are young, you are worth loving. I am neither.

PHOCION: How strange!

LEONTINA: I admit, I was granted a little beauty when it was shared out, nature left me with some charms though I have never relied on them. They may make you one day regret them; even though I say this to my shame, they are no longer there, at least the little I have left will soon go.

PHOCION: Your words are useless Leontina. You cannot convince my eyes that they can see what is not there. Is that how you hope to persuade me? Have you ever been more lovely?

LEONTINA: I am no longer what I was.

PHOCION: Let us stop here now, madam, let us argue no longer. Yes, I agree, as charming as you are your youth will pass and I will still have mine. But our souls are the same age. You know what I ask of you. I shall press Hermocrates and I will die of pain if you do not look favourably on me.

LEONTINA: I no longer know what I should do. Here comes Hermocrates now. I will stay here and decide.

(*Enter HERMOCRATES, AGIS, HARLEQUIN.*)

HERMOCRATES: (*To AGIS.*) Is this the young man you spoke to me about?

AGIS: Yes.

HARLEQUIN: I gave him your compliments while we were awaiting your arrival.

LEONTINA: This is none other than Phocion's son. His admiration for you has brought him here, he loves wisdom, and travels to improve himself. Many great men have allowed him to stay with them, he hopes for the same welcome from you. He asks for it with such urgency that he shouldn't be refused. There, I have done it. I will leave you together…ah! (*She exits.*)

AGIS: And if my approval is worth anything I will add it to Leontina's. (*He exits.*)

HARLEQUIN: And I'll throw mine in for good measure.

HERMOCRATES: (*Examining PHOCION.*) Well! Well! Well!

PHOCION: I am honoured by their entreaties on my behalf.
But you must judge me for yourself, my Lord.

HERMOCRATES: Sir, I thank you for the honour you do me.
A pupil like you would seem to have no need for a teacher
like me. However in order to judge the case better I would
like to ask you a few questions in private. (*To HARLEQUIN.*)
Leave us.

(*Exit HARLEQUIN.*)

HERMOCRATES: Perhaps I am mistaken, sir, but don't I know
you?

PHOCION: Me my Lord!

HERMOCRATES: I had my reasons for wanting to speak to
you in private. I have suspicions which are best not made
public. I wish to spare you that.

PHOCION: What kind of suspicions?

HERMOCRATES: Your name is not Phocion.

PHOCION: (*Aside.*) He remembers me from the forest.

HERMOCRATES: Phocion is in Athens.

PHOCION: Maybe it's someone with the same name as me.

HERMOCRATES: That's not all. The assumed name is only a
small part of your deceit.

PHOCION: I don't understand.

HERMOCRATES: Confess, madam, these are not your own
clothes. I saw you earlier.

PHOCION: (*Pretending to be surprised.*) You are right my Lord.

HERMOCRATES: Those prevarications were futile. But at least
you need only blush in front of me.

PHOCION: My blushes do me an injustice. I disown them. I
am not ashamed of my disguise. It has a purpose.

HERMOCRATES: Well I can see what this purpose is. It is
nothing to be proud of. You have come to entrap Agis, to
tempt him, to wound his heart so that he won't recover.
You should blush, madam.

PHOCION: Agis? Who? The young man who was here earlier?
Are these your suspicions? What have I done to arouse
them? Do you get these ideas from my face? You think my
feelings would attract him? The gods know my intentions,

they cannot let me be misunderstood. No, seigneur, I have not come here to disturb Agis' heart. Even though he was brought up by you and given strength from your teachings, no disguise would have been needed for him. Had I loved him I would have won his heart with much less effort. I would only have had to appear before him. My eyes would have spoken to him. His youth would have made him vulnerable. But I don't want his heart. The heart I seek is more difficult to catch, it is immune to the power of my eyes, and my attractions are nothing to it. I place no reliance on them and so I conceal them under my disguise where they will be of no use to me.

HERMOCRATES: But, madam, why do you want to stay here if you have no interest in Agis?

PHOCION: What? Still Agis? My Lord, please do not insult me. However things may seem, don't misjudge me. My quest may not be innocent but it is good. I hope my courage will banish your suspicions. I hope you will be impressed when you understand my motives. Enough of Agis. I repeat, I care nothing for him. Do you want conclusive proof? I don't wish to denigrate my sex, but I come here without vanity nor artifice. I come here with dignity. You have your suspicions but two words will destroy them. Will the man I love give me his hand? Here is mine. Agis is not here…

HERMOCRATES: (*Embarrassed.*) I don't know who you are talking to.

PHOCION: You do know my Lord, I have just told you. I cannot explain any better than by saying your name, Hermocrates.

HERMOCRATES: Me, madam?

PHOCION: You have been told my Lord.

HERMOCRATES: (*Disconcerted.*) So it would seem. What you have said has stunned me. How will I ever recover? Me? The object of affection of someone like you?

PHOCION: Seigneur, listen to me. I must explain myself.

HERMOCRATES: No, madam, I cannot listen any longer, all your explanations are pointless. But you have nothing to fear from me. Set your mind at rest on that score but please leave me. I was not made to be loved. Mine is a solitary and unsophisticated soul to which love is a stranger. My manner must repel your youth and charms. My heart can offer you nothing.

PHOCION: What? I am not asking for my feelings to be reciprocated. I have no hopes of that and if I ever did, I reject them. But please allow me to finish. I told you that I love you. Do you want me to suffer the pain of not being allowed to explain myself?

HERMOCRATES: My mind tells me not to listen anymore.

PHOCION: But I have compromised my pride and my virtue, and they beg me to continue. Listen to me. To be worthy of you is all I seek, the only prize my heart desires. What prevents you from listening to me? I have nothing to fight you with. My charms are undermined by the confession I made to you. They are all I have to fight with. You scorn my weakness.

HERMOCRATES: I would still prefer to pay no attention.

PHOCION: Yes, I love you but make no mistake, this is no ordinary desire. I did not make my confession by accident, I made it on purpose. Not for love but for virtue. I tell you that I love you because I need the humiliation of saying it. Because that humiliation may help me cure myself. Because I need to blush at my weakness in order to conquer it. I hurt my pride so that I might turn against you. I do not tell you that I love you so that you will love me in return. It is so that you may teach me not to love you. You hate and scorn love; I accept that. I want to be like you. Teach me to throw away my heart and resist the attraction I have for you. I do not ask to be loved but I cannot help wanting to be in love. Rid me of my desire. Protect me from you, I beg you!

HERMOCRATES: Well, madam, I will help you, hear me. I do not want to love you. I hope my indifference cures you. This conversation is poison, let us end it.

PHOCION: Good god, is that the best you can do? I had anticipated indifference. I have fearlessly exposed myself to you. Can you in your wisdom not help me?

HERMOCRATES: I will not, madam.

PHOCION: Well so be it, but give me time to soften you. Allow me to continue.

HERMOCRATES: (*Still moved.*) What now?

PHOCION: Listen to me. I have heard people speak of you, your name is known far and wide.

HERMOCRATES: Please, madam, enough of that.

PHOCION: Excuse me. My heart delights in praising what it loves. My name is Aspasia and like you I lived in solitude, my own mistress. I am very wealthy, ignorant of love and scornful of any attempt to inspire it in me.

HERMOCRATES: I should not be listening.

PHOCION: In this solitude I met you, walking alone like me and though I did not know who you were at first, just seeing you moved me. My heart found you, Hermocrates.

HERMOCRATES: I can't bear this. In the name of the virtue you cherish, Aspasia, let us end this conversation, what are you trying to do?

PHOCION: What I say may seem frivolous to you, but there is nothing frivolous about my need to return to sanity.

HERMOCRATES: And my need not to lose mine. That is of even greater concern to me. I may be naïve but I have eyes, you have charms and you love me.

PHOCION: You say I have charms? My Lord, are you afraid that you might enjoy them?

HERMOCRATES: I do not wish to expose myself to the fear.

PHOCION: If you avoid my charms, you must be afraid of something. You don't love me yet but you are afraid of loving me. You will love me Hermocrates. I don't know how to stop myself from desiring it.

HERMOCRATES: You frighten me, I can't answer you properly so I will say no more.

PHOCION: Very well, let us go and join Leontina. I want to spend some time here and you will tell me this afternoon what you have decided to do about it.

HERMOCRATES: Very well, let us go then, Aspasia, I shall follow you.

(*Exit PHOCION.*)

HERMOCRATES: I thought I would completely lose control of myself – what should I do? Come here Dimas.
(*Enter DIMAS.*)
You see the young stranger who has just left me? I order you to observe his actions and to follow him everywhere to see if he tries to engage in conversation with Agis, do you understand? I have always respected your loyalty and you could not prove it better to me than by doing exactly what I have asked you.

DIMAS: No sooner said than done, I will bring you his every thought.

Act Two

(*HARLEQUIN, DIMAS.*)

DIMAS: Come here petal. Since these newcomers arrived I never get to talk to you, whispering in corners with that mousy little valet.

HARLEQUIN: I'm just being polite, my friend, I don't like you any less.

DIMAS: But it's not polite to be rude to me. I'm your old friend. The older the friendship the better, like wine.

HARLEQUIN: A very good comparison, we'll have a few drinks later on me.

DIMAS: On you? Is it raining money?

HARLEQUIN: Don't worry yourself about it.

DIMAS: You may be a dung-heap, but I'm not stupid.

HARLEQUIN: Since when am I a dung-heap?

DIMAS: I may not know where your little windfall comes from but I saw you counting it this afternoon.

HARLEQUIN: That's right, I was doing my accounts.

DIMAS: (*First words aside.*) That's a bit desperate. Listen old tulip! Our master is in a state, there's something going on.

HARLEQUIN: Why, did he see me doing my accounts too?

DIMAS: Pouff! It's a lot worse than that. He's very suspicious of those two trespassers. He wants a fox to nose out their real intentions. He doesn't trust them an inch. I'm the one. Do you get it?

HARLEQUIN: Not really! Does this mean I'm talking to a fox?

DIMAS: Shush, keep your voice down. Listen to me! You mustn't let on about the fox to those people.

HARLEQUIN: You take care of yourself my boy.

DIMAS: Don't worry about me. I've been picking up their gossip. Nothing gets past me.

HARLEQUIN: So, you know who they are then?

DIMAS: Know who they are? Do I know the plants in this garden?

HARLEQUIN: Oh, I thought I was the only one who knew who they were.

DIMAS: You? You don't know anything.

HARLEQUIN: Oh don't I?

DIMAS: I reckon not, it's beyond you.

HARLEQUIN: Well listen to this you stubborn fool, the ladies themselves told me who they were.

DIMAS: What do you mean?

HARLEQUIN: That they are ladies!

DIMAS: (*Astonished.*) They're ladies?

HARLEQUIN: Didn't you know?

DIMAS: No, I had no idea but I do now!

HARLEQUIN: You rat!

DIMAS: So they're ladies! I'm in clover!

HARLEQUIN: I'm a complete idiot.

DIMAS: This is going to create pandemonium! I'm going to enjoy telling this one! Excellent!

HARLEQUIN: Dimas, you're cutting my throat.

DIMAS: That's your problem. Ha ha! So these ladies were bribing people behind my back, even though I was the one who caught them trespassing in his garden. This is much more important than your bleeding throat. They have got to be punished.

HARLEQUIN: Wait, are you fond of money?

DIMAS: It would be strange if I wasn't. Where is it then?

HARLEQUIN: I'll get the lady to pay for my blunder, I promise.

DIMAS: Getting you off the hook doesn't come cheap, I warn you.

HARLEQUIN: I know very well how expensive it is.

DIMAS: Just tell them I know everything. So, how much did you get off her? How much money did she give you? Tell the truth.

HARLEQUIN: She gave me twenty gold pieces.

DIMAS: Twenty pieces of gold! Good! This story is obviously worth a few sous. So, go on, what's this lady up to?

HARLEQUIN: She lost her heart to Agis when she was out walking.

DIMAS: Did he take care of it for her?

HARLEQUIN: So she dressed herself up to sneak her way into his heart without him noticing.

DIMAS: Great, I can make a good bit out of this if I move fast. So this little valet Hermidas, is she a crook too?

HARLEQUIN: I wouldn't mind taking care of that particular heart myself.

DIMAS: It won't suit you. But here we go, they're coming. Give us an advance.

(*Enter PHOCION, HERMIDAS.*)

HERMIDAS: (*Speaking to PHOCION.*) He's over there talking to the gardener. We can't speak to him.

DIMAS: They're afraid to come near us – tell 'em I know who they are.

HARLEQUIN: (*To PHOCION.*) Madam don't be angry with me, but I have been a bit indiscreet.

PHOCION: Who are you speaking to Harlequin?

HARLEQUIN: It's not good, the game's up, he tricked me into talking.

PHOCION: You wretch, you told him who I was?

HARLEQUIN: The lot.

PHOCION: Oh heavens.

DIMAS: I know all about losing your heart and how you were sneaking your way in to get Agis'. I know all about his money though I haven't found out how much of it he's promised to me.

PHOCION: Corina, it's all over.

HERMIDAS: No, madam, don't worry. You need workers to carry out your plans, so all you need to do is win over the gardener, isn't that right Dimas?

DIMAS: I'm in complete agreement with you, mademoiselle.

HERMIDAS: So what will it take?

DIMAS: Enough to buy me what I want.

HARLEQUIN: He isn't worth a sou.

PHOCION: That's all? Dimas, take this for now in advance and if you keep quiet you will thank heaven for the rest of your life that you played a part in this adventure. You are luckier than you could ever imagine.

DIMAS: Madam, I'm sold!

HARLEQUIN: And I'm ruined because of my blasted tongue. That money would have ended up in my pocket.

PHOCION: I will make you both rich. But we must discuss what brought me here and my problem. This afternoon Hermocrates promised that I could stay here for some time, but I am afraid that he may have changed his mind. He is now deep in conversation about me with Agis and his sister who also wants me to stay. Tell me the truth Harlequin, you haven't accidentally told him anything about my designs on Agis? I must know, hide nothing from me.

HARLEQUIN: No, on my life, my good lady. It was only that peasant who tricked me.

DIMAS: You'll have to learn to keep your mouth shut.

PHOCION: If you said nothing, I fear nothing. Corina will tell you what I am up to with the philosopher and his sister, and Corina, since Dimas is now on our side, share out the tasks between him and Harlequin. The first job is to see how things are working out between the brother and sister.

HERMIDAS: We will, don't worry.

PHOCION: Agis is coming. Go quickly all of you and be careful. Hermocrates must not catch us together.

(Exit DIMAS, HERMIDAS, HARLEQUIN.)

(Enter AGIS.)

AGIS: I have been looking for you, dear Phocion. I am worried. Hermocrates is no longer so disposed to you staying here. I have never been angry with him until today. He puts forward no reasonable arguments and it is not only me pressing your case, I was there when his sister spoke on your behalf. She left no stone unturned to persuade him. I don't know how it will turn out. Dear Phocion, urge him again, I beg you, as a friend. I will speak to him myself and together we can persuade him.

PHOCION: You beg me Agis? Does that mean that my being here gives you pleasure?

AGIS: When you have gone there will be nothing but boredom.

PHOCION: Only you keep me here.

AGIS: So your heart shares the same feelings as mine?

PHOCION: A thousand times more than I know how to tell you.

AGIS: Then give me some proof. This is the first time I have known the delights of friendship. You have the first fruits of my heart. Do not teach me the pain of losing a friend.

PHOCION: Me? Teach you, Agis? How could I without being its victim too?

AGIS: Your reply moves me. Let me go on. Do you remember that you told me that it would be up to me if I wished to continue seeing you? Well if that is still the case, that is my wish.

PHOCION: Ah!

AGIS: For reasons that I will tell you one day, I cannot leave this place. Phocion, you are master of your own destiny: wait here until I can determine mine. Live near us. This is a solitary place but we will be together; and what sweeter thing can the world offer than the gentle mingling of two virtuous hearts?

PHOCION: Yes I promise, Agis. After what you have just said my whole world is here where you are.

AGIS: I am very happy. The gods cursed my birth but now you have said that you will stay it means they must have been appeased: your presence is a sign of their favour.

PHOCION: Agis, at this great moment of pleasure in seeing you so moved, I am still afraid. Love could alter such delicate feelings. A friend cannot compete with a lover.

AGIS: What? Me in love? Phocion, may heaven make your soul as inaccessible as mine! You don't know me. My education, my feelings, my mind have closed my heart to love. It was love that caused my family's misfortune and I despise it. I despise the sex which inspires it in us.

PHOCION: You hate that sex Agis?

AGIS: I have fled from it all my life.

PHOCION: That changes everything between us, sir. Although I promised to live in this place, I cannot in good faith. It is no longer possible. I will leave. One day you may have cause to reproach me, I don't want to deceive you so I return to you the friendship you have given me.

AGIS: What do you mean, Phocion? Why have you changed? What did I say to displease you?

PHOCION: Agis, you will not miss me. You are afraid to know the pain of losing a friend. I will soon experience it but you will not.

AGIS: Me, stop being your friend?

PHOCION: You are still mine, seigneur, but I am no longer yours. I am one of the objects of your hatred that you spoke of just now.

AGIS: What, you mean you aren't Phocion?

PHOCION: No, seigneur, these clothes are a lie. They conceal an unfortunate girl who has escaped from the Princess' persecution. My name is Aspasia and I was born into a famous family of which I am the last. The fortune I inherited is the reason for my flight. The Princess wants me to marry one of her relations who loves me, though I detest him. So I escaped in this disguise. I had heard of Hermocrates and the retreat in which he lived and I came to him for a short time at least, to find refuge. Then I met you, you offered me your friendship. I saw that you were worthy of mine. The truth that I have told you is the proof of my friendship and I will keep to it despite your hatred.

AGIS: I don't know what to think.

PHOCION: I shall do the thinking for you. Goodbye, sir. Hermocrates wants me to leave, my presence causes you pain. My departure will satisfy you both. I will go in search of good people who will not refuse me refuge.

AGIS: No, madam, stop. It's true that your sex is dangerous, but I cannot ignore your unhappiness.

PHOCION: You detest me, sir.

AGIS: No, I tell you, stay, Aspasia. You are in a pitiful state. I should have been more sensitive. I will entreat Hermocrates to allow you to stay, your unhappiness demands it.

PHOCION: So you will only act out of pity for me. How sad this makes me. The man they wish me to marry now seems very attractive. Would it not be better to give myself to him rather than go on like this?

AGIS: I do not advise it, madam, marriage must go with love.
I have heard that the saddest fate is to be united with
someone one doesn't love. Life becomes an eternity of
sorrow and even virtue makes us wretched. But perhaps
you feel that you might come to love the man who is
intended for you?

PHOCION: No, sir, my flight from him is proof of that.

AGIS: Take care unless some secret desire draws you to
another – that would be even worse.

PHOCION: No I tell you, I am just like you. Until now my
heart has known nothing except for the friendship I had for
you and if you leave me that, I will never want to have any
other feeling.

AGIS: (*Embarrassed.*) Well then do not return to the Princess
because I still feel the same way.

PHOCION: So you still like me?

AGIS: Still, madam, and so much that there can be nothing to
fear. There is only friendship between us, that is the only
emotion I can inspire and the only one, no doubt, you are
capable of feeling.

PHOCION / AGIS: (*At the same time.*) Ah!

PHOCION: Sir, no one is worthier than you to be called a
friend. The word 'lover' is not for you, though I should not
say so.

AGIS: I never want to be called it.

PHOCION: Let us leave love well alone, it is too dangerous
even to speak of it.

AGIS: (*Somewhat embarrassed.*) I think a servant is coming to
look for you. Perhaps Hermocrates is no longer busy, allow
me to leave you and go and join him.

(*Exit AGIS.*)

(*Enter HARLEQUIN, HERMIDAS.*)

HARLEQUIN: Well Madam Phocion, three sentries to guard
your tête-à-tête. You should be impressed.

HERMIDAS: I haven't seen Hermocrates but his sister is
looking for you. She asked the gardener where you were.
She seems a little sad, apparently the philosopher is not
giving in.

PHOCION: Oh, he'll give in or the arts of my sex are worth nothing.

HARLEQUIN: And what about Agis, has he promised nothing? Is his heart simmering a little?

PHOCION: One or two more conversations and I'll have it.

HERMIDAS: Seriously, madam?

PHOCION: Yes Corina, you know the reasons for my love. The gods are already signalling my reward.

HARLEQUIN: I hope they won't miss out my reward, they can see how honest I am.

HERMIDAS: (*To HARLEQUIN.*) Quiet, I see Leontina, let us hide.

PHOCION: Have you told Harlequin what needs to be done now?

HERMIDAS: Yes, madam.

HARLEQUIN: You'll be charmed when you see how good I am.

(*Exit HARLEQUIN, HERMIDAS.*)

(*Enter LEONTINA.*)

PHOCION: I was coming to find you, madam, I have been told what is going on. Hermocrates is going back on his word to me. I am in terrible distress.

LEONTINA: Yes Phocion, Hermocrates is being irrational and obstinate. He refuses to keep his word to me. You are going to tell me that I must press him again. I must tell you that I will do nothing of the kind.

PHOCION: You will do nothing of the kind Leontina?

LEONTINA: No, his refusal has brought me back to my senses.

PHOCION: You call this coming back to your senses? What? My love must be clouding my understanding. I was coming to tell you that I will never be cured. I yearn to touch you and now you want me to leave? No Leontina, it is not possible, it is a sacrifice that my heart cannot make. Leave you? Where do you think I can find the strength? What have you done to me? Look at the state I'm in. I appeal to your Virtue. I implore it to judge between you and me. I am in your home, you have allowed it. You know that I love you: look at me, ravished by the most tender passion. You have inspired it in me. How am I supposed to leave?

Leontina, ask for my life, tear out my heart, they both belong to you. But do not ask me for what I cannot give.

LEONTINA: Such passion! Oh such passion! No Phocion you must go. I must be free of this. Oh heaven. My heart cannot cope with yours. I cannot bear your passionate words. I must fight them and resist them. They must never be allowed to conquer. No Phocion, you want me to feel love but I only feel the pain of being in love. Go, I beg you and leave me be.

PHOCION: Please spare me Leontina. The idea of leaving you terrifies me. I don't know how to live without you, I will flood this place with my despair, I no longer know where I am!

LEONTINA: You want me to love you because you are unhappy? That is tyranny!

PHOCION: So you despise me?

LEONTINA: I ought to.

PHOCION: But did your heart respond to mine?

LEONTINA: I don't want to hear.

PHOCION: But I can't give you up.

LEONTINA: Stop, I hear someone.

(*Enter HARLEQUIN. He slips silently between the other two.*)

PHOCION: What is your servant doing, madam?

HARLEQUIN: Lord Hermocrates has ordered me to keep an eye on you because he knows nothing about you.

PHOCION: But I'm with Madam; surely you don't need to spy on me? (*To LEONTINA.*) Tell him to leave, madam, I beg you.

LEONTINA: It would be better if I left myself.

PHOCION: (*In a low voice to LEONTINA.*) If you go without promising to speak on my behalf I shall not be able to answer for my actions.

LEONTINA: (*Moved.*) Ah! (*To HARLEQUIN.*) Go Harlequin, you needn't stay here.

HARLEQUIN: Indeed I must, you have no idea who you are dealing with. This gentleman is not interested in cleverness, only in clever girls. I warn you he has designs on your innocence.

LEONTINA: (*Signalling to PHOCION.*) What do you mean
Harlequin? Do you have any proof? Surely you are joking?

HARLEQUIN: No, no, no. Listen, madam, this afternoon
his valet, another villain, came to talk to me. So, can we
be friends? Oh, with all my heart. How lucky you are
to be here. It's not too bad. How honest your master is!
Wonderful. How kind your mistress is. Oh, divine. So, tell
me, has she had any lovers? As many as she wants. Will
she have any more? As many as she wants. Does she want
to marry? She doesn't tell me. Will she stay a spinster? I
couldn't guarantee it. Who does she receive? Who doesn't
she receive? Who visits her, who doesn't visit her, and so
on and so forth. Is your master in love? He has lost his
heart, the only reason we are staying is to get it back and
marry her. He has enough money and passion to fill ten
palaces.

PHOCION: Haven't you said enough?

HARLEQUIN: That's upset him. He could tell you a lot more.

LEONTINA: Admit it, Phocion, Hermidas was only joking?
(*PHOCION does not answer.*)

HARLEQUIN: (*Clears his throat.*) Your voice is very faint, my
dear mistress, perhaps someone is trying to steal your
heart. It is being threatened as we speak. I shall get Lord
Hermocrates to come to your rescue.

LEONTINA: Stop Harlequin, I don't want him to know that we
were talking about love.

HARLEQUIN: Oh well if the robber is a friend of yours there's
no point in crying thief. Wisdom is flexible. Get married,
she won't be kicked out. Being a good wife has its merits.
Adieu, madam, do not forget your little servant who will
keep his mouth shut.

PHOCION: Go, I'll pay you for your silence.

(*Exit HARLEQUIN.*)

LEONTINA: This is a bad dream. What are you doing to me?
Who's coming now?
(*Enter HERMIDAS.*)

HERMIDAS: (*Carrying a portrait which she gives to PHOCION.*) This
is what you wanted sir. Are you pleased with it? It would
have been better if I had worked from the actual person.

PHOCION: Why have you brought me this in front of Madam? Well let's see. Yes, the face is good, that noble and refined air. But what about the fire in the eyes?

LEONTINA: You are talking about a portrait sir?

PHOCION: Yes, madam.

HERMIDAS: Give it back to me sir, I'll take account of what you've said.

LEONTINA: May I look before you take it away?

PHOCION: It's not finished, madam.

LEONTINA: If there is a reason for not showing it to me I shall not insist.

PHOCION: Here it is, madam. Please give it back to me.

LEONTINA: Me!

PHOCION: I never want to lose you from my sight. The slightest separation is painful to me even if it lasts only a moment. This portrait gives me comfort. But keep it if you like.

LEONTINA: I should not return it but your love makes me feel weak.

PHOCION: Take mine in return. Then I shall always be with you. What's the matter? Doesn't my love inspire you a little?

LEONTINA: (*Sighing.*) It shouldn't but I am not in control.

PHOCION: You make me so happy.

LEONTINA: And if I loved you?

PHOCION: Not if, tell me you do.

LEONTINA: (*Still moved.*) It is the truth Phocion!

PHOCION: Then I will stay. You will speak to Hermocrates?

LEONTINA: Yes, I need time to make up my mind about our marriage.

HERMIDAS: Quiet, I see Dimas coming.

LEONTINA: I am so overwhelmed I don't wish anyone to see me. *Au revoir*, Phocion, I will get my brother's consent.

(*Exit LEONTINA.*)

(*Enter DIMAS.*)

DIMAS: Here comes the philosopher walking in a daze. Leave me some room to transplant him.

PHOCION: Good luck Dimas, I'll come back when he has left.

(*Exit PHOCION and HERMIDAS.*)

(*Enter HERMOCRATES.*)

HERMOCRATES: Have you seen Phocion?

DIMAS: No, but I've got a lot to tell you about him.

HERMOCRATES: Have you discovered something? Is he with
    Agis a lot? Is he trying to see him?

DIMAS: Oh no, he has plenty of other plants bedded.

HERMOCRATES: (*First words aside.*) I'm afraid to hear the rest.
    What do you mean?

DIMAS: It means you are a great man, you're wise, you're
    virtuous and you look good.

HERMOCRATES: What are you so worked up about?

DIMAS: I'm comparing your face with the face of a certain
    visitor. Extraordinary things are happening that have never
    happened to you, because someone here is going about,
    dying, sighing. Alas, they say, how I love that dear man,
    that lovely man!

HERMOCRATES: I don't know who you are referring to.

DIMAS: I refer to you. There's worse, all this is coming from a
    boy who is in fact a girl.

HERMOCRATES: I don't know anyone like that.

DIMAS: You know Phocion? Well, it's only his clothes that are
    a man, all the rest is a girl.

HERMOCRATES: What are you telling me?

DIMAS: And she's not short of charms! You are a lucky man.
    Do you know who these charms are intended for? I've
    heard them talking, they're saying that they are being
    saved up for the most perfect mortal found amongst all
    mortal men, his name is Hermocrates.

HERMOCRATES: Who, me?

DIMAS: Believe me.

HERMOCRATES: (*Aside.*) What more is he going to say?

DIMAS: While I was following your orders this afternoon I
    saw him cutting through the wood with his valet Hermidas
    who is a boy/girl like him. I crept near them and I heard
    them talking. Phocion starts – 'Ah Corina, it is all over,
    there is no cure for me. I love that man too much, I no
    longer know what to do or say.' 'But, madam, you are so
    beautiful.' 'What good is this beauty since he wants me to

leave?' 'Be patient, madam.' 'But where is he, what is he doing? What's happened to his wisdom?'

HERMOCRATES: (*Moved.*) Stop Dimas.

DIMAS: I've nearly finished. 'But what did he say to you when you spoke to him, madam?' 'Well he scolded me, I can't bear it my dear. He tells me he is wise. So am I. But I pity you he says. So do I, I say. Aren't you ashamed he says? Where would that get me I say? But what about your virtue, madam? But what about my torment my Lord? Shouldn't two such virtues be joined?'

HERMOCRATES: I've had enough of this, enough.

DIMAS: If you want my advice, master, you could cure that child by falling ill like her and marrying her. Staying a bachelor severs a man's roots and it would be a shame to cut yours off. While you're at it could you fix me up with the chambermaid? I'm all for sowing seeds.

HERMOCRATES: (*First words aside.*) That's all I need! Be discreet Dimas, I order you. She would be upset if she knew about this. I'll sort it out when I see her again... Ah!

(*Exit HERMOCRATES.*)

(*Enter PHOCION.*)

PHOCION: So Dimas, where's Hermocrates got to?

DIMAS: He's going to let you stay.

PHOCION: Excellent.

DIMAS: But he isn't going to let you stay.

PHOCION: I don't understand.

DIMAS: He hasn't the slightest idea what he wants. He actually said that his philosophy was worthless, that he only has an ounce left.

PHOCION: He won't have that for much longer. It took a portrait to deal with his sister's squeamishness and I've got another one to use on the brother. I can't be bothered to invent something new. I think Agis is avoiding me. I haven't seen him since he found out who I am. He was speaking to Corina earlier on, perhaps he is looking for me?

DIMAS: Good guess, here he is. Don't forget, madam, the real
    end of this adventure is I get to make my fortune.

PHOCION: You can count on it.

DIMAS: Thanks to you.

                                      (*Exit DIMAS.*)

   (*Enter AGIS.*)

AGIS: Aspasia, why do you run away from me?

PHOCION: Because this afternoon I saw that you were running
    away from me.

AGIS: I admit it, I was, something was worrying me and still is.

PHOCION: May I know what it is?

AGIS: There is a person who I like but I don't know if what I
    feel for her is friendship or love. I am only a beginner to all
    this and I was coming to ask you to instruct me.

PHOCION: Perhaps I know this person.

AGIS: That's not difficult. When you came here, you knew that
    I loved no one.

PHOCION: Yes and since I have been here you have only seen
    me.

AGIS: You can draw your own conclusions.

PHOCION: It must be me.

AGIS: Yes, it is you, Aspasia. Tell me what my feelings are.

PHOCION: I don't know. Tell me what my feelings are, I am in
    the same situation with someone I love.

AGIS: Who is that, Aspasia?

PHOCION: Who is it? The same reasons which led you to
    conclude that you loved me apply to me. Can't you work it
    out for yourself?

AGIS: You had never loved when you came here.

PHOCION: I am no longer the same and I have only seen you.
    The rest is clear.

AGIS: Then your heart aches for me, Aspasia?

PHOCION: Yes but what does it mean? We loved each other
    before we worried about it, so is our love now the same or
    different? That's the question we must answer.

AGIS: If we tell each other what we feel, perhaps that will help.

PHOCION: Let's try. Did it hurt you to avoid me?

AGIS: It was infinitely painful.

PHOCION: That's bad. Were you avoiding me because your heart was tormented by feelings that you did not dare tell me about?

AGIS: You understand me perfectly.

PHOCION: Yes. But I warn you it's no good for your heart. And looking at your eyes, it doesn't seem very good for them either.

AGIS: They look at you with overwhelming pleasure, a pleasure beyond any ordinary emotion.

PHOCION: Enough, it's love. No further questions.

AGIS: I'd give my life to you, I'd give a thousand lives if I had them.

PHOCION: More proof. Love in your expression, love in your emotions, in your eyes, love if ever it was.

AGIS: Love as never before perhaps. But I have told you what's happening to my heart. Can I know what's happening to yours?

PHOCION: Gently, Agis, a person of my sex may speak of friendship as much as she wants but never of her love. Besides you are already too vulnerable, too moved by your emotions. If I told you my secret you might be even worse.

AGIS: Your eyes have already spoken to mine. You are not immune.

PHOCION: Oh, well I can't speak for my eyes, they may tell you that I love you but I haven't said so.

AGIS: Your words fill me with delight and passion. Your feelings are the same as mine.

PHOCION: Yes, you've guessed in spite of me. But it's not enough to love. It mustn't be secret it must be shouted to the world. But Hermocrates is in charge of you, and…

AGIS: I respect and love him. But I already know that hearts have no master. I must see him before he speaks to you because he may well send you away today and we need a little time to decide what we should do.

DIMAS: (*Appears in a corner of the theatre without approaching and calls out to warn them to finish their conversation.*) Ta ra ta la ra.

PHOCION: Agis, let us part for now. We must see each other soon. I have many things to tell you.

AGIS: Me too.

PHOCION: Let us leave. I am afraid that if we are seen together too much people will guess who I am. *Au revoir.*

AGIS: I shall leave you, my lovely Aspasia, and I will make sure you stay here. Hermocrates may be free now.

(Exit AGIS.)

(Enter HERMOCRATES, DIMAS.)

DIMAS: (*Speaking rapidly to PHOCION.*) It's a good thing he's gone. Look who's coming.

(Exit DIMAS.)

PHOCION: At last Hermocrates. I know you are doing this to weaken my desire but you can't imagine the pain it causes me. It makes me sad but it doesn't lessen my tenderness.

HERMOCRATES: Various matters kept me away Aspasia but there can no longer be any question of desires. Your stay here is not practical now, it would be wrong for you. Dimas knows who you are. Need I go on? He knows your heart's secret. He overheard you and we can't trust his discretion. For the sake of your pride you must leave.

PHOCION: Leave? You can't send me away in this state. I have a thousand more problems than I had before. What have you done to cure me? Is this what you call virtuous help?

HERMOCRATES: I hope what I am going to tell you will solve your problems. You thought I was wise, you loved me because of it but I have lost my wisdom. A true wise man would have used his virtue to secure your peace of mind. But do you know why I'm sending you away? It's because I'm frightened that your secret will become public and destroy my reputation. I am sacrificing you not because I am virtuous but because I can't bear other people to think I'm not virtuous. I am nothing more than a vain and arrogant man to whom wisdom is not important provided the world thinks me wise. There, this is the object of your love.

PHOCION: I have never admired you so much.

HERMOCRATES: Why?

PHOCION: Ah sir, are these the only tricks you can use against me? You admit your shame because of your weakness, and yet all this does is make me more vulnerable. You say that you are not wise. And yet you give me sublime proof to the contrary.

HERMOCRATES: Wait, madam. Did you believe that I might not be susceptible to the havoc that love wreaks in the hearts of other men? The basest soul, the crudest lovers, the most foolish youths have not experienced the torment that I have felt. Worry, jealousy, passion tear me apart. Is this the Hermocrates you imagined? The universe is full of people like me. Stop loving me. Any man chosen at random would deserve your love as much as I do.

PHOCION: No, no, no. If the gods could be weak they would be like Hermocrates! Never was he greater, never more worthy of my love and never was my love so worthy of him! You speak of my pride – what has that to do with the least of the emotions of which you speak? No, seigneur, I will no longer ask you for my heart's desire, you have given it to me by your confession. You love me. I am contented. I am ravished. You have guaranteed our union.

HERMOCRATES: There is only one thing left for me to do. I will reveal your secret, I will dishonour the man you admire. His offence will contaminate you if you do not leave.

PHOCION: Well I am leaving. But I am safe from vengeance. Because you love me your heart will protect me. I am in despair. You are running away from a love that would bring happiness to your life and so you will bring unhappiness to mine. Enjoy your wretched wisdom. My misfortune will last for ever. I came to ask you for help against my love. You've done nothing except to confess that you love me. And after that confession you send me away, after a confession which doubles my affection! The gods will despise that wisdom. It has broken a young heart that you have tricked, whose confidence you have betrayed, whose virtuous feelings you have not respected and which has been the victim of your vicious philosophy.

HERMOCRATES: Please keep your voice down, madam, the others are coming.

PHOCION: You destroy me and you expect me to be quiet?

HERMOCRATES: You have affected me more than you think but please calm down.

(*Enter HARLEQUIN, HERMIDAS.*)

HERMIDAS: (*Running after HARLEQUIN.*) Give it back to me! You have no right to keep it? What are you doing?

HARLEQUIN: Don't strain my loyalty, I must warn my master.

HERMOCRATES: (*To HARLEQUIN.*) What is this noise for? What's the matter? What does Hermidas want?

HARLEQUIN: Treachery. A pact between the devil and his minions. It must be made public.

HERMOCRATES: Explain yourself.

HARLEQUIN: I have just found this young man sitting, apparently writing. He was dreaming, nodding his head, looking his work and then I noticed that he had a palette by him on which he had grey, green, yellow, white and he was dipping his brush into it. I tried to see what he was writing but he's a villain. There were no words or phrases, he was writing a face and the face was yours.

HERMOCRATES: Me!

HARLEQUIN: Your very own face except that it is a bit smaller than your actual nose. Surely you're not allowed to shrink people's noses in paintings? Look at the face he's given you. (*He gives him a portrait.*)

HERMOCRATES: You have done well, Harlequin, I will not rebuke you. Go, I want to find out what this means.

HARLEQUIN: They'd never fit your real nose into that tiny little frame!

(*Exit HARLEQUIN.*)

HERMOCRATES: What were you thinking of? Why have you painted me?

HERMIDAS: For a very simple reason, my Lord. I wanted the portrait of a famous man. I wanted to show it to other people.

HERMOCRATES: You do me too great an honour.

HERMIDAS: And I knew that the portrait would give pleasure to a certain person who would never ask for it.

HERMOCRATES: So, this person, who is she?

HERMIDAS: Sir…

PHOCION: Keep quiet, Corina.

HERMOCRATES: What do you mean, Aspasia?

PHOCION: Do not ask any more, Hermocrates, please leave it.

HERMOCRATES: What exactly do you want me to ignore?

PHOCION: Stop this, you are making me blush.

HERMOCRATES: I can hardly believe my own eyes. I don't know what is happening to me. It's like a dream.

PHOCION: This is beyond dreaming.

HERMOCRATES: This is the proof. It is too much for me.

PHOCION: Corina, why did you let yourself be found out?

HERMOCRATES: You have won, Aspasia, take it, I give in.

PHOCION: I forgive you for the embarrassment my victory causes me.

HERMOCRATES: Take back this portrait, it belongs to you, madam.

PHOCION: No I will never take back what your heart rejects.

HERMOCRATES: You must take it back.

PHOCION: (*Pulls out her own portrait and gives it to him.*) My own may please you a little. Here it is, take good care of it. Then I will be with you for ever.

HERMOCRATES: (*His mouth near her.*) Haven't you humiliated me enough? I will argue with you no longer.

HERMIDAS: It isn't quite finished. If the Lord Hermocrates would just allow me, it'll only take a minute or two.

PHOCION: There's no one here. It'll only take a minute. Don't refuse her.

HERMOCRATES: Aspasia, don't expose me to that risk, someone might catch us.

PHOCION: You say this is my moment of victory. We must not waste it, it is precious. Your eyes are looking at me with a tenderness that I want to capture in your portrait. You cannot see your own expression, it is so charming. Finish it Corina, finish.

HERMIDAS: My Lord, just a bit to the side I beg you, allow me to see you properly.

HERMOCRATES: Oh God, what have you reduced me to?

PHOCION: Does your heart blush at the gift it gives me?

HERMIDAS: Lift your head a little.

HERMOCRATES: Do you want me to Aspasia?

HERMIDAS: Turn to the right a little.

HERMOCRATES: Stop, Agis is coming. Go Hermidas.

(*Exit HERMIDAS.*)

(*Enter AGIS.*)

AGIS: My Lord I have come to beg you to allow Phocion to stay for a while but I suppose that you will not consent to it and that there is no point in me speaking to you.

HERMOCRATES: (*In a worried tone.*) So you hope that he will stay Agis?

AGIS: I confess I would be very sad if he left and that nothing would give me so much pleasure than for him to stay here. To know him is to admire him and friendship follows easily from admiration.

HERMOCRATES: I didn't know that you were so intimate with each other.

PHOCION: Actually we have not had many chances to talk.

AGIS: Perhaps I have interrupted your conversation and that may be the reason for your coldness towards me. I shall leave.

(*Exit AGIS.*)

HERMOCRATES: What does Agis' persistence mean? I don't know what to believe. Since he has been with me I have never seen him so interested in anyone as he is with you. What do you know about him? Have you told him who you are? Are you taking advantage of me?

PHOCION: I am overwhelmed with joy. You are jealous! The only thing left to me was the pleasure of seeing it for myself and you have given it to me. You wrong me but I am grateful. Hermocrates is jealous, he cherishes me, he adores me. He may be unfair but he loves me, what does it matter if he is unjust? But I must clear myself. Agis is not far away I can still see him. Let him return, let us call him back my Lord. I will look for him myself, I will speak to him and you will see whether your suspicions are well founded.

HERMOCRATES: No, Aspasia, I recognise my mistake, your frankness reassures me, do not call him back, I give in. The others still do not need to know that I love you. Give me time to sort everything out.

PHOCION: Of course. Here's your sister. I will leave you together. (*Aside.*) I pity his weakness. God, pardon my deceit.

(*Exit PHOCION.*)

(*Enter LEONTINA.*)

LEONTINA: There you are, dear brother, I have been asking everyone where you were.

HERMOCRATES: Why do you want me, Leontina?

LEONTINA: What have you decided about Phocion? Do you still intend to send him away? This afternoon he showed such admiration for you and spoke so well that I promised him that he could stay and that you would agree. I gave him my word, he won't stay long. You must not go against me.

HERMOCRATES: No Leontina, you know that I have a high regard for you and I would never go against you. Since you have promised, there is nothing more to say. He can stay as long as he wishes, dear sister.

LEONTINA: Thank you for your kindness, dear brother. Phocion deserves our help.

HERMOCRATES: I know his worth.

LEONTINA: Besides he will amuse Agis. It is not right that he should be alone at his age.

HERMOCRATES: At any age.

LEONTINA: You are right, we all have moments of sadness. If I may have the courage to say it, I am often tired of loneliness myself.

HERMOCRATES: What do you mean 'courage'? Who doesn't weary of it? Were we not born to be sociable?

LEONTINA: We don't know what we do when we hide ourselves away. Perhaps we were hasty when we chose such a harsh life.

HERMOCRATES: Dear sister, it's too late for such thoughts.

LEONTINA: Why? There is a cure for the illness. One can change one's mind.

HERMOCRATES: That's quite true.

LEONTINA: A man of your age would be welcomed anywhere should he wish to change his state.

HERMOCRATES: And you are lovelier and younger than me. I have no fear for you either.

LEONTINA: Yes brother, few young people can compare with you. The gift of your heart would not be rejected.

HERMOCRATES: And I assure you the same would be true of your heart, should you offer it.

LEONTINA: So you wouldn't be surprised if I had such plans?

HERMOCRATES: I would be surprised if you did not.

LEONTINA: But what about you?

HERMOCRATES: Eh, who knows, perhaps I have.

LEONTINA: The gods invented marriage. Who are we to question them? I believe that a contemplative man would make a good husband. Think about it. We will talk again. *Au revoir.*

HERMOCRATES: I have some orders to give, then I will follow you. (*Aside.*) Clearly Leontina and I are both in a good state. I wonder who she wants. Perhaps someone young just as I have Aspasia. How weak we are. But we must not avoid our destiny.

Act Three

(*PHOCION, HERMIDAS.*)

PHOCION: Come here, I want to talk to you, Corina. I think we will be completely successful. I need one more tiny conversation with Agis. He wants it as much as I do. We haven't quite managed it. Hermocrates and his sister have plagued me in turn. They both want to marry me in secret. I don't know how many plans have been made for these imaginary weddings. It is beyond belief how this so-called wisdom can be unhinged by love. I have to listen to it endlessly until I finally win Agis. I know he loves me dearly as Aspasia. Will he hate me as Leonida?

HERMIDAS: No, madam, go for the kill. After all she has done, the Princess Leonida will appear even more wonderful than Aspasia.

PHOCION: I agree with you but his family did die at the hands of mine.

HERMIDAS: Your father inherited the throne and he spared Agis' life.

PHOCION: I know. I feel both love and fear. But I shall act as though I was certain of success. Did you take my letters to the chateau?

HERMIDAS: Yes, madam. Dimas, who I kept in the dark, provided a man and I gave them to him. It's not far from here to the palace so you'll soon have some news. What have you asked Ariston in the letters?

PHOCION: I told him to follow the person who gave them to him, to come here with his guards and my entourage. I want Agis to leave here as a prince. I'll wait here. You go to the entrance to the gardens. Warn me as soon as Ariston arrives. Go. You have done me fine service. This is the finale.

HERMIDAS: I'm going. But you've still got Leontina to deal with. She's looking for you.

(*Exit HERMIDAS.*)

(*Enter LEONTINA.*)

LEONTINA: I have just a quick word to say to you dear
Phocion. The die is cast. Our troubles will soon be over.

PHOCION: Yes, thank heavens.

LEONTINA: I have taken control of my life. We are going to
be united for ever. I know the marriage can't happen here,
but the plans we have made don't seem quite respectable
to me. You have sent for a carriage which will wait for
us some distance from the house. Would it not be better,
instead of us leaving together, that I should leave first and
wait for you in town?

PHOCION: Yes, you're right, well thought.

LEONTINA: I shall go immediately and prepare myself for that
and in two hours' time I shall not be here. Phocion, follow
me as quickly as you can.

PHOCION: The quicker you go, the quicker I can follow you.

LEONTINA: Love is everything.

PHOCION: Everything, but don't let it distract you now.

LEONTINA: You are the only person in the world who could
make me do this.

PHOCION: It is blessed. You run no risk. Go and prepare for it.

LEONTINA: I love your urgency, may it last for ever!

PHOCION: Try to be the same. Your dawdling makes me
impatient.

LEONTINA: Every now and then I feel so sad.

PHOCION: Why? I feel nothing but joy.

LEONTINA: Do not be impatient. I am leaving. My brother is
coming. I don't want him to see me at this moment.

(*Exit LEONTINA.*)

PHOCION: Not again! Will I never be rid of him?
(*Enter HERMOCRATES.*)
Hermocrates, I thought you were busy making
arrangements for your departure.

HERMOCRATES: Ah, delightful Aspasia, if you only knew the
battle going on inside me.

PHOCION: Ah, if you only knew how weary I am of
your battles. What do you mean? You are difficult to
understand.

HERMOCRATES: Forgive these palpitations. My heart is trying to be strong.

PHOCION: Your heart is certainly trying, Hermocrates. Never mind your palpitations. You don't want to get married here, so you must leave.

HERMOCRATES: Ah!

PHOCION: That sigh won't get anything done.

HERMOCRATES: I have one more thing to tell you but I am very embarrassed about it.

PHOCION: You always have one more thing.

HERMOCRATES: Can I confide in you completely? I have abandoned my heart to you, I am going to be yours so I have nothing more to hide from you.

PHOCION: Go on.

HERMOCRATES: I brought Agis up from the age of eight. I can't leave him so soon. Please allow him to live with us for a while. Let him join us later.

PHOCION: Why?

HERMOCRATES: Our interests are as one. I shall tell you my great secret. You have heard of Cleomenes. Well, Agis is his son, kidnapped from prison in his infancy.

PHOCION: Your secret is safe with me.

HERMOCRATES: You can see how carefully I have hidden him. Imagine what would become of him if he fell into the hands of the Princess? She has been looking for him. She wants him dead.

PHOCION: I've heard that she is generous and fair.

HERMOCRATES: I don't trust her, she comes from a family which certainly isn't.

PHOCION: They say that she would marry Agis if she ever knew him, especially as they are of the same age.

HERMOCRATES: She might well want to marry him but the hatred he has for her would prevent it.

PHOCION: Surely the glory of pardoning one's enemies is greater than the honour of hating them for ever, especially when those enemies are innocent of the wrongs that have been done.

HERMOCRATES: If there wasn't a throne at stake you would be right but there is. There can be no question of him forgiving her.

PHOCION: It would make Agis happy.

HERMOCRATES: He won't stay with us for very long. Our friends are preparing for war with the enemy. He will join them. Things are moving fast. We will soon see great changes.

PHOCION: Will they kill the Princess?

HERMOCRATES: She is merely the descendant of guilty men. To kill her would be committing one crime in revenge for another and Agis is not capable of that. It will be enough to defeat her.

PHOCION: Well, I think you've told me everything. Go and prepare yourself to leave.

HERMOCRATES: *Au revoir*, dear Aspasia, these are my last hours here.

(Exit HERMOCRATES.)

(Enter HARLEQUIN, DIMAS.)

PHOCION: When will this be over? I believe Agis wants to speak to me. The idea of his hatred makes me weak. What do these servants want now?

HARLEQUIN: I am your servant, madam.

DIMAS: I greet you, madam.

PHOCION: Not so loud.

DIMAS: Don't worry, we are alone.

PHOCION: What do you want from me?

HARLEQUIN: Just a trifle.

DIMAS: Yes I'm here just to get things straight.

HARLEQUIN: And to see how things are going.

PHOCION: What is this about? Be quick, I am in a hurry.

DIMAS: Right, as my friend says we've done a good job for you?

PHOCION: Yes, you have both served me well.

DIMAS: Is your plan working?

PHOCION: I have one more thing to say to Agis. He is waiting for me now.

HARLEQUIN: Good, since he is waiting for you, we won't talk long.

DIMAS: Let's talk business. I have done some dangerous and dastardly things. I have been incredibly brave.

HARLEQUIN: We are the best scoundrels in the world.

DIMAS: I've had to stifle my conscience which was extremely difficult and that alone is worth a great deal.

HARLEQUIN: One moment you were a boy which wasn't true. The next moment you were a girl and what else I don't know.

DIMAS: First you love one, then another. I've helped your heart capture everyone else's. My assistance was invaluable.

PHOCION: Have you finished? Where is all this taking us?

HARLEQUIN: Then there's their portraits that you gave away for nothing when you could have got real money for them.

DIMAS: Your play will soon be finished. How much are you going to give us for the last act?

PHOCION: What do you mean?

HARLEQUIN: Buy the rest of the drama – we'll sell it to you for a reasonable price.

DIMAS: Do business with us or I'll spoil everything.

PHOCION: Did I not promise to make your fortunes?

DIMAS: Yes but put your money where your mouth is.

HARLEQUIN: Yes because when there's nothing left to do, scoundrels tend to get badly paid.

PHOCION: My children, you are insolent.

DIMAS: Oh that's good.

HARLEQUIN: We agree we are insolent.

PHOCION: You are annoying me. This is my response. If you destroy me, if you are not discreet, I will make you pay for your indiscretion in a dungeon. You don't know who I am. I warn you I have the power to do this. If, on the other hand you keep quiet, I will keep all the promises I gave you. You choose. I order you to leave. Correct your error by obeying me at once.

DIMAS: (*To HARLEQUIN.*) What will we do, dandelion? She frightens me, should we go on being insolent?

HARLEQUIN: No, that might lead us to the dungeon and I can't think of anything I like less than four prison walls. Let's go.

(*Exit DIMAS, HARLEQUIN.*)

(*Enter AGIS.*)

PHOCION: (*Aside.*) That shook them. Agis is here at last.

AGIS: So I have found you again, Aspasia. At last I have a moment to speak freely to you. I am going through torture! I nearly came to hate Hermocrates and Leontina for the friendship they showed you. But who could not love you? How lovely you are Aspasia and how sweet it is to love you.

PHOCION: How happy I am to hear you say that Agis. You will know very soon how highly I prize your heart. But tell me, that tenderness whose innocence charms me, is it absolute proof of your love? Is there anything that could steal it away from me?

AGIS: No, I would only lose you by dying.

PHOCION: I have not told you everything Agis, you still do not know everything about me.

AGIS: I know your charms, I know the sweetness of your soul, nothing could tear me away from them. I will adore you for the rest of my life.

PHOCION: Oh God, what love. It becomes dearer to me moment by moment. So does the fear that when you find out my birthright I may repel you.

AGIS: Alas, you don't know who I am either. I am afraid of uniting my fate to yours. Oh cruel Princess, how many reasons I have to hate you.

PHOCION: Eh? Who are you talking about Agis? Which princess do you hate so much?

AGIS: The princess who reigns here, Aspasia, my enemy and yours. Someone is coming, I can't go on.

PHOCION: It's Hermocrates. I hate him for interrupting us. I'll only leave you for a minute Agis and I'll come back as soon as he's gone. Our destiny together depends on only one word. You hate me without knowing why.

AGIS: Me, Aspasia?

PHOCION: I haven't time to tell you any more. Get rid of Hermocrates.

(*Exit PHOCION.*)

AGIS: I don't understand what she means. Hermocrates mustn't suspect anything.

(*Enter HERMOCRATES.*)

HERMOCRATES: Wait, Prince, I must speak with you. I don't know where to start.

AGIS: Why are you so embarrassed?

HERMOCRATES: You could never imagine. I am ashamed to admit it to you but it is better that you should know.

AGIS: Tell me. What has happened to you?

HERMOCRATES: I am as weak as the next man.

AGIS: What kind of weakness are you talking about, seigneur?

HERMOCRATES: The most excusable one in the whole world, the most common but the least expected by me. You know what I think about that passion that is called love.

AGIS: Yes, you've always exaggerated.

HERMOCRATES: Yes, that may be but what can I do? A solitary man like me who meditates, studies, deals only with his mind and never with his heart, a man imprisoned in his austerity is hardly in a position to make a judgement about such things. He will always go too far.

AGIS: There's no doubt about it, you have always gone too far.

HERMOCRATES: You are right. I think like you. Didn't I tell myself that? How mad this passion was, extravagant, unworthy of a reasonable man. I called it delirium but I don't know what I was saying. It had nothing to do with reason or nature. I was criticising heaven.

AGIS: Yes, in the end we are all made to love.

HERMOCRATES: Exactly so. It makes the world go round.

AGIS: And it might well take revenge on you one day for scorning it.

HERMOCRATES: Your threat comes too late.

AGIS: Why is that?

HERMOCRATES: I have already been punished.

AGIS: Seriously?

HERMOCRATES: I will tell you everything. I am about to change my life. If you love me, you will come with me. I am leaving today to be married.

AGIS: That's why you're embarrassed?

HERMOCRATES: It is not a pleasant thing to go back on one's word. In my case it is a long journey.

AGIS: I congratulate you. All you needed to make you complete was to know your heart.

HERMOCRATES: I have learned my lesson. If you knew what it took to trap me, how strong her love must have been, how it inspired her to brilliant trickery, you would think me ungrateful not to have responded sooner. Wisdom abhors ingratitude and I was oh-so-nearly ungrateful. She had seen me several times in the forest. She took a liking for me, she tried to stop it but she could not. She resolved to speak to me but she was intimidated by my reputation. So she disguised herself, she changed her clothes and became the most handsome of men, arrived here and we met. I wanted her to leave, as I believed that it was you she was interested in. She swore to me that she was not. To convince me she told me she loved me. Could I doubt her, she asked. 'My hand, my fortune, are all yours along with my heart. Give me yours or cure mine. Give in to my feelings or teach me to conquer them. Give me back my indifference or share my love.' And she told me all this with her charms, with her eyes, with a tone of voice that would have conquered the wildest of men.

AGIS: (*Concerned.*) But my Lord, this passionate lover who disguised herself, have I met her here? Is she here?

HERMOCRATES: She is.

AGIS: But I can only see Phocion!

HERMOCRATES: That's who it is but don't say a word, here comes my sister.

(*Enter LEONTINA.*)

AGIS: (*Aside.*) She is a destroyer! Why has she tricked me?

LEONTINA: I have come to tell you that I shall be making a little trip to the town dear brother.

HERMOCRATES: Who are you visiting, Leontina?

LEONTINA: Phrosina. She says she has some news for me.

HERMOCRATES: Well then we shall both be absent because I am also leaving within the hour. I was speaking to Agis about it.

LEONTINA: And who will you be visiting?

HERMOCRATES: Just visiting Criton.

LEONTINA: In town like me! It is quite unusual for us both to have business there. Do you remember what you said to me this afternoon? Is there some mystery about your journey?

HERMOCRATES: Yes I remember what you were telling me too. Am I right in suspecting the real reason for your trip?

LEONTINA: Hermocrates, let us speak with open hearts. The truth is I am not going to see Phrosina.

HERMOCRATES: And the truth is, I am not going to see Criton.

LEONTINA: My heart has decided where I'm going.

HERMOCRATES: So has mine.

LEONTINA: Well then I must tell you I am to be married.

HERMOCRATES: Well, so am I.

LEONTINA: That is good Hermocrates. Now that we have told each other, the man I love and I don't have to go. He is here and since you now know everything, there's no point in our being married elsewhere.

HERMOCRATES: You're right. I shan't leave either. We shall be married together because the lady to whom I'm giving myself is also here.

LEONTINA: Please tell me who she is? I will tell you, I am betrothed to Phocion.

HERMOCRATES: Phocion!

LEONTINA: Yes, Phocion.

HERMOCRATES: Who? The one who came to find us here? The one you were talking to me about this afternoon?

LEONTINA: Yes.

HERMOCRATES: But I'm marrying him. We can't both marry him.

LEONTINA: You are marrying him? Are you dreaming?

HERMOCRATES: Not at all.

LEONTINA: What does this mean? Phocion loves me with
an infinite tenderness. He even had my portrait painted
without me knowing and gave me his to keep.

HERMOCRATES: Your portrait? It isn't yours, it is mine.

LEONTINA: But you're wrong. Here is his portrait, do you
recognise it?

HERMOCRATES: This is its double, sister; the only difference is
that yours is of a man and mine a woman.

LEONTINA: Oh my God!

AGIS: I can't bear it any longer. She didn't give me a portrait
but I too am to marry her.

HERMOCRATES: You Agis, what do you mean for God's sake?

LEONTINA: This is intolerable.

HERMOCRATES: We're wasting time. This is a plot and our
servants are part of it. Come with me Leontina, that girl
must be made to explain herself and her deception.

(*Exit HERMOCRATES, LEONTINA.*)

(*Enter PHOCION.*)

AGIS: (*Without seeing PHOCION.*) I am in utter despair.

PHOCION: Thank God they've gone. What is wrong, Agis,
won't you look at me?

AGIS: Why did you come here? Which of the three of us do
you plan to marry, Hermocrates, Leontina or me?

PHOCION: I understand. I have been found out.

AGIS: Aren't you going to give me your portrait like you did
the others?

PHOCION: The others have had only portraits. You have the
actual person.

AGIS: I don't know your real name so *adieu* traitor, *adieu* for
ever. I want to die.

PHOCION: Stop, dearest Agis, listen to me.

AGIS: Leave me alone.

PHOCION: No I will not leave you. If you don't listen to me
you will be the most ungrateful of men.

AGIS: Me? But you deceived me!

PHOCION: Because of you I deceived everyone and I had
to. My deceit was evidence of my love. You are, without
knowing, slandering the truest heart there ever was. I am

not trying to pacify you, you don't know how much love
you owe me or the love I have for you. You will love me,
you will admire me, you will ask my pardon.

AGIS: I don't understand.

PHOCION: To win your heart I had to abuse others. It was the
only way. Everything I have done is for you.

AGIS: How can I believe you, Aspasia?

PHOCION: Dimas and Harlequin know my secret. They have
been working for me and they will confirm the truth of
what I'm telling you. You must ask them. I can't bring
myself to.

AGIS: Is this really possible, Aspasia? Then no one has ever
loved me as much as you.

PHOCION: That isn't all. There is still the Princess who you
call our enemy.

AGIS: If you love me, one day she will turn that love to grief.
She hates me. Only my death will satisfy her.

PHOCION: I can give you control of her destiny.

AGIS: I do not ask anything of her except to allow us to lead
our own lives.

PHOCION: Decide her destiny for yourself. Her heart sets you
free.

AGIS: Her heart? You mean that you are Leonida, madam?

PHOCION: I told you that you didn't know the extent of my
love. Now you do.

AGIS: (*Falls to his knees.*) I do not have words to express mine
to you.

(*Enter LEONTINA, HERMOCRATES.*)

HERMOCRATES: What's this? Agis on his knees? (*They
approach.*) Who is this portrait of?

PHOCION: Me.

LEONTINA: And this one, traitor?

PHOCION: Me. Do you want me to swap them for yours?

HERMOCRATES: How can you joke? Who are you? What are
you trying to do?

PHOCION: I am going to tell you. But allow me to speak with
Corina first.

(*Enter HERMIDAS, DIMAS, HARLEQUIN and the rest of the actors.*)

DIMAS: Master I warn you, there's a whole lot of men with axes at the bottom of our garden and soldiers and golden carriages.

HERMIDAS: Madam, Ariston has arrived.

PHOCION: (*To AGIS.*) Your Highness, come and receive the homage of your subjects. It is time to leave. Your guards are waiting for you. (*To HERMOCRATES and LEONTINA.*) You Hermocrates and you Leontina who both refused to allow me to stay, understand why I deceived you. I wanted to return the throne to Agis and I wanted to be his. My real name would have repelled him and so I disguised myself to take him unawares. I would not have succeeded had I not taken advantage of you both. Hermocrates, you will have nothing to complain about, your mind will take care of your heart. Leontina, now you know my sex all your passion will surely disappear.

THE GAME OF LOVE AND CHANCE

Translated and adapted
by Neil Bartlett

Introduction

What follows is the script as it stood at the end of the second week of rehearsal. When originally delivered to the company, it came with the following explanatory notes.

The Time

The play – the game of the title – takes place in two historical periods simultaneously: then and now. (This is of course true of any new production of an old play). The 'then' of our production is sometime in the middle 1930s; the 'now' is the night of the actual performance. The language of the script is rooted in a theatricalised memory of the 1930s – but the performers, since they are contemporary actors, not just 'real' 1930s people, are also allowed and obliged to quote other theatrical styles – they sometimes seem to be grabbing quotations off the dressing room rail of theatre history and using them as they see fit. At times this may create the effect that they are improvising, not acting.

The Place

Onstage is a 1930s interior representing the reception room of an upper-class family house – panelled walls, a telephone, an ashtray, a grand piano: the bare necessities of civilised life. There are five doors: one leading to the main staircase of the house; one leading to the guest rooms; and three discreetly concealed staff doors. This onstage area is governed by the strict rules of pre-war etiquette. Offstage there is all the usual paraphernalia – props tables, mirrors, worn out armchairs, old copies of newspapers, packets of Silk Cut, dirty coffee mugs. (Again, this is the set-up for most productions of old plays. The only difference here is that in our production both areas are visible to the audience.)

The Script

My suggestions of possible non-verbal actions are exactly that: suggestions. It does seem to me crucial that we see some of the encounters that the text itself does not describe.

The punctuation of Marivaux is very difficult to understand on the page. Sometimes it is used to give a very specific shape to lines, and sometimes it is much more shapeless – the characters just talk and talk with endless semi-colons to indicate pauses for breath. The punctuation of the translation should therefore be taken with great care: sometimes it is there for precise effect; sometimes I have used dashes or semi-colons to indicate pauses that may end up being commas, dashes or even full stops depending on the performer's taste and instincts. All opportunities allowed by the period language for eccentricities of stress should be extravagantly exploited.

Nationality

Arlecchino is Italian, and English is his second language. Lisette is English (we may be sure that her real name isn't Lisette: she only uses that name in her professional capacity as coiffeuse). Marivaux's Mario has become Maurice, because I didn't want anyone to wonder why he wasn't Italian. Monsieur Orgon has become Mr Prowde and Dorante has become Mr Dorant. Silvia is Silvia.

Repetitions

You will see that I have proposed several places where text is repeated. This is my own invention, but is inspired by the original. Characters are always reusing words and lines from earlier scenes in their dialogues; they themselves often attempt to go back to the beginnings of scenes and start again, and in the extraordinary speech which Silvia makes describing Dorante's exit in the third act Marivaux himself seems to propose a speech which is that of an actor meditating on and replaying a theatrical moment, rather than that of an actor pretending to talk like a real person in real life. Some of the repetitions reflect my own experience of translating the play, in that they offer different readings of the same line. All of these repetitions are optional.

The original production was cast before this translation was made, and each part was written for a particular performer. This influenced the production in three crucial ways. Firstly, any production of the play must recognise that the role of Arlecchino can properly only be played by a real Harlequin, not an actor. Anyone who wants to do it must find their own distinctive solution to this problem. The Arlecchino in the first production was Marcello Magni, who played Marivaux's text in several languages simultaneously; Italian, English, French, Mime and Slapstick were prominent. Where his lines are printed [in square brackets] this indicates that I have provided a literal translation of the French which must then be used by the performer concerned as the basis for his performance. Secondly, the role of Maurice was treated very distinctively (high-handedly), because it was written to be played by a singer-pianist. He played most of his scenes (and several others) seated at the grand piano, which was in the centre of the set, providing appropriate (or devastatingly inappropriate) accompaniment to the action – in the form of either set-piece songs, or the apparently random but in fact very pointed tinklings of a dressing-gowned, chain-smoking 1930s queen. Thirdly, our Silvia was considerably older than our Dorant. We weren't interested in making a show about the confusions of an *ingénue* – we wanted to make a show about just how much someone who has very good reasons to be single has to lose when they fall in love with someone in every way unsuitable.

This script contains echoes of other scripts and I would like you to be aware of these as you are reading. Coward (*The Vortex* and *Brief Encounter*), Congreve (*Love for Love*) and old scripts for *Upstairs Downstairs* were much in my mind as I wrote.

This translation would not have been possible if Mr James Gardiner had not made me understand what Silvia means when she says, 'Ah, now I see how my heart works'. My thanks to him for that, and for listening patiently to all of the first four versions of the script in their entirety.

Neil Bartlett

Characters

MR PROWDE
The Father. A Widower

SILVIA
The Daughter. A Society Woman

MAURICE
The Brother. A Bachelor

LISETTE
The Maid. A distant relative of that 'thoroughly
experienced French maid' referred to by Lady
Bracknell in *The Importance of Being Earnest*

MR DORANT
The Suitor. An Eligible Young Man,
recently down from College

ARLECCHINO
The Chauffeur. An Italian

The Suitor's name is pronounced 'Durrant'.

This translation of *The Game of Love and Chance* was first performed in October 1992. The production was commissioned and co-produced by Gloria and the Cambridge Theatre Company in association with the Royal National Theatre. The cast was as follows:

SILVIA, Maggie Steed

LISETTE, Caroline Quentin

MR PROWDE, Trevor Baxter

MAURICE, Stefan Bednarczyk

MR DORANT, Peter Wingfield

ARLECCHINO, Marcello Magni

Directors Mike Alfreds and Neil Bartlett

Designer Paul Dart

Movement Leah Hausman

Music Nicolas Bloomfield

A piano is being played.

We see four men – THE FATHER, THE BROTHER, THE SUITOR and THE CHAUFFEUR. Seen as a quartet, they seem ominous, even sinister. They seem very definitely a quartet, a team, a foursome.

We also see THE MAID, going about her business, and clearly not having anything to do with them. If there are sides in this game then she is definitely not on theirs.

We then see SILVIA, absolutely on her own. She has her back to us; when she turns we see that she is perfectly dressed and perfectly made up. One gets the impression that she has already had several cups of coffee. Either she is dying for a cigarette or she is smoking one. Not only does she have to deal with what her maid has just told her, she has to deal with an audience as well.

SILVIA makes her own rather free but nonetheless accurate translation of Monsieur Marivaux's opening line. She says: WHAT THE HELL HAS IT GOT TO DO WITH YOU? and then, immediately, the play begins.

Act One

SCENE 1

(*Morning.*

We jump-cut straight into the middle of a conversation. Throughout this conversation, LISETTE is at work with coffee cups, dressing gowns, clothes, ashtrays et cetera, the morning routine, continually exiting and entering.)

SILVIA: Alright, I'll say it again; you had no right to interfere. Since when did *you* answer for *my* feelings?

LISETTE: I did think that on this one particular occasion your feelings might resemble those of every other woman in the world. The Master your father asked me if you were reconciled to the idea of his wanting to get you married, if you relished the prospect; and so I said yes I said. Well obviously I did. And quite possibly you're the only single woman in the entire world in regard to whom The Yes wouldn't be the right answer. The No isn't natural.

SILVIA: 'The No isn't natural.' What a ridiculous line. I take it that you find the prospect of marriage utterly charming.

LISETTE: Definitely The Yes once again.

SILVIA: That'll do. Go and exercise your impertinence elsewhere – and in future, it is not your place to judge my heart according to the workings of yours.

LISETTE: My heart's made just like everybody else's. I don't see why yours has taken it into its head to be made like nobody's.

SILVIA: Honestly, if she had the nerve, she'd come right out with it and call me a...an eccentric.

LISETTE: If she had your money we'd soon see.

SILVIA: Lisette, you are trying to be trying.

LISETTE: I was hardly trying at all. I don't see what great harm there was in me telling him you don't mind the idea of getting married.

SILVIA: Firstly...you didn't quite tell the truth. I am *not* bored with being single.

LISETTE: News to me.

SILVIA: It is, secondly, not appropriate that my father should think his idea of marrying me off gives me any great pleasure, since that may lead him to pursue it with a confidence that may well prove groundless.

LISETTE: What? You're not going to marry the one he's picked you?

SILVIA: How should I know? Perhaps he won't be to my taste – that's why I'm so tense.

LISETTE: I heard he's a real gentleman – well spoken, well dressed. Well built. I heard you couldn't possibly get one who had a better temper or a better sense of humour; what more d'you want, sounds to me like the ideal husband.

SILVIA: 'The Ideal Husband'. Where do you acquire these expressions?

LISETTE: Lord knows, madam, it's rare enough for a gentleman of his quality to want to do things properly these days; if he came round courting most women of my acquaintance would have him without standing on any sort of ceremony. Well put together, that's what you need in private; well mannered and well spoken, that's what you need when you're out in Society. Practical and decorative: he's got the lot.

SILVIA: Yes he has, pictured like that, and one hears it's quite a good likeness, but one only hears, and when one sees one mayn't concur in the general verdict. Apparently he is singularly good looking, which I find rather unattractive in a man.

LISETTE: Well that's a very modern idea.

SILVIA: It's a very sensible idea. How often one has remarked on the vanity of the handsome.

LISETTE: Oh he's wrong being vain but he's alright being handsome.

SILVIA: And they do say he's got a terrific physique. Oh well –

LISETTE: Oh well yes I'm sure we could forgive him that.

SILVIA: Handsome, distinguished – I find it all so very superficial.

LISETTE: Yes madam, well if I ever get married, I assure you I shall find it all very necessary.

SILVIA: You don't know what you're talking about. In marriage, one requires the reasonable, not the desirable. Actually, all I'm looking for is decency, and that's harder to find in a man than people think. This one comes highly recommended; but I don't know anyone who's actually sampled the goods. Men are so prone to making false claims about themselves. Especially the clever ones. And I should know, knowing as I do the most eligible men in town. It's all so charming, so very reasonable, so very amusing, they all look as smart as indeed one finds they are. 'He looks a decent sort, such a dependable, solid sort', one used to hear that all the time about Tom. 'Well he is,' people used to say. I myself used to say: 'What you see is what you get with Tom.' Oh yes, there's a face one can trust, so charming, so considerate, so easily transformed a quarter of an hour later into that of an aggressive boor who terrorises an entire household. Tom got married: and now that's all his wife, his children and his staff ever see of him, while he still goes about town parading the friendly physiognomy by which we all recognise him and which is in fact nothing but a mask he puts on with his hat whenever he leaves the house.

LISETTE: How peculiar to have two faces.

SILVIA: And doesn't everyone take one look at Dick and instinctively adore him? Well, in the privacy of his own home the man never utters a word, never laughs, never even lets slip a sigh; he's not so much incommunicative as inert: ice, inside. His own wife has no idea what's going on in his head; they never talk; she's married to a kind of frigid recluse who only ever leaves his study to come down to dinner – at which he then makes the whole table simply die of depression, chilliness and boredom. What fun that must be.

LISETTE: I'm catching a cold hearing you describe him. And what about that Harry?

SILVIA: What about that Harry? The other day they had had some sort of a row; I called; I was announced, and I watched him come down to greet me with open arms, charm itself; from the way he was smiling one would have thought I had merely interrupted some quite inconsequential conversation. The beast. That's what men are like. One would never have known that his wife was in tears. Over him. I found her in a complete state, white as a sheet, eyes ruined with all that weeping. I found her in the sort of state in which I may one day find myself. I recognised my future self in that portrait, my probable destiny as a cheap reproduction. I felt sorry for her, Lisette: imagine, one day, you may feel sorry for me. What an appalling idea. So there you have him. 'The Husband.' What do you think?

LISETTE: 'The Husband.' Is a husband. It was a mistake to end up with that word because it's made me forget all the rest. (*Enter MR PROWDE.*)

SCENE 2

PROWDE: Good morning, daughter. I trust you'll find the news to your liking…your young man arrives this morning; his father has just informed me of as much in this letter. 'But answer came there none.' … You look unhappy. And Lisette looks at the floor. Now what's all that about? You tell me then Lisette; what is the matter?

LISETTE: Oh sir, one face that gives you the shakes, another that makes you catch your death; one set of insides (frozen) that keep themselves very much to themselves, oh and of course the depressed portrait with the white sheet and the red eyes; that, sir, is the matter we have been working so hard at getting ourselves into a state over.

PROWDE: What is she talking about? Insides, portraits, someone'll have to explain, it's all beyond me.

SILVIA: I've been entertaining Lisette with 'The Misfortunes of The Unhappily Married Woman' – I cited the case of Harry's wife, who I found the other day horribly depressed because her husband had just shouted at her; I was simply making a few observations on that topic.

LISETTE: Ah yes, friendly physiognomies; we were observing that The Husband wears a mask for work and a frown for the wife.

PROWDE: From which, I take it, I am to understand that the prospect of marriage, daughter, alarms you – and all the more so because you have not met the young man in question.

LISETTE: Firstly, he's good looking, which is a real shame.

PROWDE: A shame? Lisette, are you feeling quite well this morning? A shame?

LISETTE: I only speak as I'm spoken at; that's Madam's theory and I'm sticking to it.

PROWDE: Yes well never mind all that now. My dear, you know how much I love you. Mr Dorant is coming here to court you – now I made this arrangement when I was last down in the country, where his father is my oldest and my dearest friend – but it was made on the condition that the pair of you get on; I forbid you to make any allowance for my feelings in this matter. If he isn't to your liking, then you just say the word, he'll be sent packing; and if you shouldn't be to his – well back he goes just the same.

LISETTE: Shouldn't take more than one number then:
(*LISETTE sings snatches of two popular songs of the period, one illustrating MR PROWDE's first scenario – that the pair will be well matched and will get married – and the second illustrating*

his second – that they'll be ill matched and will swiftly part.
Her contribution to the debate is ignored.)

PROWDE: I myself have never actually met this Dorant, he was
away when I was down at his father's place, but to judge by
what I'm told about him I confidently predict that neither
of you will want to send the other packing.

SILVIA: I'm touched by how sweet you're being about all of
this, Daddy. You've forbidden me to make any allowances
and I shall do exactly as you say.

PROWDE: As I insist.

SILVIA: But I was wondering, and I feel embarrassed asking
really, because I've only just thought of it, if you might
grant me one small favour; it would make me feel so much
more relaxed about the whole thing.

PROWDE: You can but ask; if it's that small, I'll grant it.

SILVIA: Oh it's minute, but I'm afraid you'll think I'm taking
advantage of how good to me you are.

PROWDE: Take it, dear girl; you know these days one has to be
a little too good to be true in order to be truly good.

LISETTE: Only a really nice man could get away with a line
like that.

PROWDE: Tell me what it is I can do for you, my daughter.

SILVIA: He's due here this morning, if only I could see him,
study him a little without him knowing it was me. Lisette is
good at charades, she could take my place for a little while,
and I could take hers.

PROWDE: What a charming idea… Allow me a moment's
consideration of your proposal. If I let her do it, the
charade may turn out to be a little more original than
she expects… Very well, my dear, I shall allow you your
change of role. Do you think you will be able to manage
yours, Lisette?

LISETTE: Me, sir, oh you know what I'm like. 'Try any chat
on with me and see where it gets you, sunshine. This
physiognomy 'ere merely 'ints at my 'igh Society ways and
means of dealing with the likes of you.' Well? What d'you
think? Recognise Lisette then do you?

PROWDE: Quite remarkable. Even I was completely taken in.
But good heavens, is that the time! – off, off and get ready

– we don't want Mr Dorant catching us unawares – haste, haste – and make sure the rest of the staff are told.

SILVIA: I really shan't need more than an apron.

(*LISETTE, who was already on her way to get to those frocks, stops in her tracks. She takes off her apron, and drops it for SILVIA to pick up. When she speaks, she does not crudely parody a caricatured Society Lady; she now mimics SILVIA, in particular and with complete accuracy.*)

LISETTE: And I really must go and see to my face; Lisette, you may as well begin to acquaint yourself with your duties by doing my hair…a little promptitude while we're working, if you don't mind.

SILVIA: (*Fighting back with an imitation of equal accuracy.*) Oh madam, I'm sure I'll soon have you sorted out. Alright? (*Exit LISETTE. Enter MAURICE.*)

SCENE 3

MAURICE: Sister dear, congratulations, I've just heard. So, we're going to *meet* this young man of yours.

SILVIA: Brother dear, yes. But I've got things to be getting on with so you will have to ask Father for all the details, do excuse me. (*Exit SILVIA.*)

SCENE 4

PROWDE: Let her go, Maurice, I can tell you all you need to know.

MAURICE: I take it there's news, pater.

PROWDE: I would just say, by way of a preface, that I am only telling you this on the understanding that I do so in complete confidence.

MAURICE: Absolutely.

PROWDE: We *are* going to meet Mr Dorant today; but we are going to meet him in disguise.

MAURICE: In disguise. Is he coming in fancy dress – oh God, you're going to give him a party.

PROWDE: …here's the relevant paragraph in the father's letter… 'Moreover I have no idea what your reaction will be to a scheme which my son has lately dreamt up – it is a little hare-brained, as even he admits – but seems to spring from honourable and even sensible motives – namely, he has requested my permission to arrive at your house disguised as his own chauffeur – who will in turn be impersonating his master.'

MAURICE: Now that will be amusing.

PROWDE: Listen to the rest – 'My son remains entirely serious about his pending engagement. He hopes, he says, while temporarily so disguised, to observe the character of his intended and to get to know her a little so that he may properly make up his mind with regard to his future – we did after all agree that he should be free to make it up for himself. Personally I trust entirely your glowing accounts of your daughter and so have consented to the whole thing while taking the precaution of alerting you – despite a request from him that I should keep you in the dark. It's up to you whether or not you tell the lucky girl herself.' And there is now an additional complication. Your sister, herself a little anxious on the subject of this Dorant – and as yet unaware of his little scheme – has requested my permission to stage her own version of the very same charade in order to observe him precisely as he wishes to observe her. Well? A rather…original situation, don't you think? Maid and Mistress are at this very minute on-ing with the motley. What would you advise, Maurice? Do I tell your sister or not?

MAURICE: Frankly, Father, if that's the lie of the land I think I should respect the happy coincidence of their having had the same idea at the same time; and indeed ensure they are provided with every opportunity to practise their mutual deception. Let's see if their hearts find each other out. Perhaps Mr Dorant will take a fancy to my sister *en soubrette* which would be charming for her.

PROWDE: Let's see her get out of this one.

MAURICE: It can hardly fail to be diverting. Personally I shall be booking a seat in the front row and offering our happy couple every possible encouragement.

SCENE 5

(*MAURICE rings the bell. Enter SILVIA.*)

SILVIA: You rang, m'sieur? How do I do as The Maid. You apparently know what's occurring, brother dear; what's your verdict?

MAURICE: I should say, sister dear, that the chauffeur doesn't have a hope in hell – and I shouldn't be at all surprised if The Maid steals The Master from under her Mistress's nose.

SILVIA: Actually I don't think I should at all mind him falling for me while I'm in character. I should quite enjoy driving him a little mad, dizzying him a little as he teeters on the edge of the social chasm yawning between us. If this can do that for me then I shall be happy – and indeed proud – to wear it. Besides it'll help me to find out what he's really like. As for his chauffeur, I hardly think I need fear any advances from that quarter; I'm sure even in this my innate refinement of feature will inspire respect rather than any nonsense from the likes of him.

MAURICE: Careful; you are now the likes of him.

PROWDE: And he is bound to find you attractive.

SILVIA: Well I'm sure I can turn that honour to my advantage; chauffeurs always love to talk; lovers talk too much, and so I shall make him tell me *all* about his master.

(*Either the phone rings, or the Stage Manager comes on – either way, LISETTE can't deliver it because she's too busy dressing up – but MR PROWDE gets the message that DORANT has arrived in disguise as his own servant.*)

PROWDE: Well send him up. Dorant's chauffeur is here. His master seems to have been delayed slightly on some business matter. Where's Lisette?

SILVIA: Lisette is dressing, and is advised by her mirror that we are most unwise to deliver Mr Dorant up to her tender mercies; she's nearly ready.

(*There is a knock at the door.*)

PROWDE: Steady on – here we go.

SCENE 6

(*They arrange themselves. Enter DORANT, carrying luggage.*)

DORANT: I'm looking for a Mr Prowde; is it to him that I have the honour of offering my services?

PROWDE: Indeed, my boy, it is.

DORANT: Sir, as I hope you have been informed, I am here on behalf of Mr Dorant, who will be following shortly, and who has sent me on ahead to assure you of his best respects until such time as he can do so in person.

PROWDE: You have taken his place most graciously. Lisette, what do you think of this lad here?

SILVIA: Me, sir, I think he is quite welcome. And quite promising.

DORANT: You are too kind. I do the best I can.

MAURICE: And quite striking, really. Let's hope your affections aren't tempted to stray from the straight and narrow, Lisette.

SILVIA: My affections, oh sir, that's quite another matter.

DORANT: Don't mind him, young lady, Sir fancies me more than I do myself.

SILVIA: How much I admire modesty in a man. Pray continue in that vein.

MAURICE: Oh, very good, one might almost think the title of 'Young Lady' were appropriate. Listen, if you people are going to be so formal with the introductions you'll be standing on ceremony all day. Let's be a bit more familiar shall we? She's Lisette, and you, dear boy, what d'you call yourself?

DORANT: Birmingham, sir, at your service.

SILVIA: Alright. 'Hello Birmingham.'

DORANT: Oh really? 'Hello Lisette.' At your service.

MAURICE: 'At your service', no, no, not at all the correct usage – try 'I'm all yours'.

(*MR PROWDE laughs.*)

SILVIA: (*To MAURICE.*) You're making a fool of me.

DORANT: If there's any call for familiarity I leave that up to Lisette here.

SILVIA: You feel free, Birmingham, go on and break the bleedin' ice if that makes the Master 'ere 'appy.

DORANT: Ta very much, Lisette, and I'm only too glad to respond to your civility in kind.

PROWDE: Never mind, my dears; perhaps you'll find yourselves falling in love, then all these social niceties will seem somehow…irrelevant.

MAURICE: Steady on; falling in love, that's quite another matter – or perhaps you are unaware of my own, personal, interest in Lisette's heart. True – it spurns me as yet – but I don't want Birmingham trespassing on my property.

SILVIA: Oh, really! Is that how you want to play it? Well I wish Birmingham would fall in love with me.

DORANT: There was really no need to have said that, Lisette; your wish is my command without you having to say a word.

MAURICE: Mister Birmingham, you must have picked that little compliment up somewhere very special.

DORANT: Indeed I did sir, I found it lying in her eyes.

MAURICE: That will do thank you; I can't abide smart remarks from the staff.

SILVIA: He's not making them at your expense; and if I've got something in my eye, then he's welcome to it.

PROWDE: I think you're losing the argument, my boy, let's go. Mr Dorant will be here at any moment, and we should inform my daughter – and you, Lisette, show this lad which is his master's room. Goodbye, Birmingham.

(*MR PROWDE shakes DORANT's hand.*)

DORANT: Sir, you're too kind.

(*Exit MR PROWDE and MAURICE.*)

SCENE 7

SILVIA: I'm glad they think this is a comedy. Still, never mind, I can turn that to my advantage; the boy's no fool, and I don't pity the maid who gets him. Now watch this; he's going to 'make conversation' with me. I'm sure I shall find it most instructive.

DORANT: What a striking girl. That profile would be a credit to any woman in Society; now to get better acquainted... Since we're bein' so familiar and the old formality's straight out the window, tell me something, Lisette, is your mistress anything like you? She must be quite a dazzler if she's got you for a maid.

SILVIA: Birmingham, this question would seem to indicate that you are now, as I understand is customary in these scenes, about to engage me in seductive conversation: is that correct?

DORANT: Good Lord no, that wasn't the plan at all. Though I am of course your typical chauffeur, I've never been much of a one for the maids; I've never cared much for the domestic banter, though of course in your case...well, that's quite a different matter. What! I'm quite overcome with you. Almost shy. I'm usually terrifically familiar but that doesn't seem the right tack with you somehow, I keep on wanting to take my hat off, and when I speak common with you I feel as though I'm just putting it on, in fact I feel instinctively as if I ought to treat you with respect: funny, really. What sort of a maid are you anyway, eh, you look like a real lady to me.

SILVIA: Oh dear, I seem to inspire precisely those same sentiments in every chauffeur I ever meet.

DORANT: And in every master too I'll bet.

SILVIA: What a well-rehearsed routine you have – but as I have already indicated, I am *not* susceptible to flattery from people with wardrobes like yours.

DORANT: Are you trying to say you don't like me in this uniform?

SILVIA: No, Birmingham. I'm not. Now, let's forget about love, and let's be friends.

DORANT: Is that all? The final line of your routine is grammatically correct but emotionally impossible.

SILVIA: (*Aside.*) What an extraordinary man for a chauffeur. Nevertheless, let us pursue that line; it was once foretold I should never get married except to a real gentleman; and

I promised not to listen to offers from any man who wasn't one.

DORANT: Good God! How extraordinary; I feel just the same way about women as you do about men; I've taken a vow never to get serious with any girl who isn't a real lady.

SILVIA: Now hardly seems the time to abandon such a lofty ideal.

DORANT: You never know, I might not be abandoning as much as one thinks; you're very distinguished-looking... perhaps you are of noble birth and know it not.

SILVIA: I would thank you for that moving little speech were it not made at the expense of my mother.

DORANT: Why not even the score with an insult aimed at mine? Or perhaps you don't think I'm distinguished-looking enough to be worth being rude to.

SILVIA: (*Aside.*) Oh you're worth it alright. But that's hardly the issue here: that's enough comic dialogue – I was promised a guaranteed gentleman and I won't settle for less.

DORANT: Lord, even if I was one, I'd find your prophecy a bit daunting: I'd be afraid of finding out I wasn't really who I thought I was. I don't believe in the stars. But I believe in your face.

SILVIA: (*Aside.*) He doesn't give up, does he? Have you quite finished? Since the stars excluded you from their calculations I don't think you should include them in yours.

DORANT: They never said I shouldn't love you.

SILVIA: No, but they did say that it wouldn't do you any good if you did, and I'm happy to be able to confirm their opinion.

DORANT: You're right of course, Lisette, Pride suits you perfectly. It was the one finishing touch you seemed to lack – I've been trying to work out what it was that was missing ever since I first saw you, and now that I've found it – though it plays hell with any plans I may have had – I can console myself with the knowledge that my loss is your gain.

SILVIA: (*Aside.*) Quite frankly, the boy's a surprise, though not
    an entirely pleasant one. Tell me, who are you, and where
    did you learn to talk like that?

DORANT: The son of a good family fallen on hard times.

SILVIA: Oh…well here's to good times just around the corner;
    I only wish there was something I could do… Lady Luck's
    been a bit rough on you, hasn't she?

DORANT: Cupid's been rougher; I'd rather have his
    permission to ask for your heart than all the tea in China.

SILVIA: (*Aside.*) Heavens, anyone would think we'd rehearsed
    this. Birmingham, I cannot bring myself to object to the
    manner of your conversation, but I would ask that we
    change the subject. How about…your master. You can not
    talk about Love, I take it.

DORANT: You could not inspire it.

SILVIA: Oh now I shall get cross. You're making me impatient.
    Change the subject.

DORANT: Change your face.

SILVIA: (*Aside.*) Actually I'm beginning to find him quite
    amusing. Well then, Birmingham, it seems you simply can't
    help yourself. In which case I shall be forced to leave you.
    Which I really should have done already.

DORANT: Wait, Lisette, there was something else I wanted to
    talk to you about. But I can't remember what it was.

SILVIA: Yes, I had something I wanted to talk to you about as
    well – but you've made me quite lose my thread too.

DORANT: I remember asking you if your mistress was
    anything like you – (*DORANT goes back a couple of pages and
    tries to start the scene again:*) Since we're being so familiar
    and the old formality's straight out the window, tell me
    something, Lisette, is your mistress as lovely as you
    are – any woman would be a fool to risk comparison with
    you –

SILVIA: Your brief detour has got you back on the same old
    track, goodbye.

DORANT: Oh, no, honestly – Lisette – this is about my master,
    really.

SILVIA: Good, I wanted to talk to you about him, I'd rather
    hoped you might be able to tell me, confidentially, what

he's like. That you're attached to him predisposes me to
like him; he can't be all bad if he's got you working for
him.

DORANT: Could I please just say how kind it was of you to say
that.

SILVIA: Would you please just ignore how foolish it was of me
to say it.

DORANT: You see – it's the way you come out with these
things that makes me feel…beside myself. Do as
you please; I find you irresistible; and I find it most
extraordinary that I am…in…servitude to one of the most
adorable creatures I have ever met.

SILVIA: And I find it most odd that I'm prepared to listen to
this sort of thing, because frankly, it's unlike me.

DORANT: You're right, the whole thing is unlikely.

SILVIA: (*Aside.*) It doesn't seem to matter what he says, I
haven't gone, I am not going. I am still here, and I am still
talking to him. Really, it's beyond a joke. Goodbye.

DORANT: Let's finish what we wanted to say.

SILVIA: Goodbye, I said; no more liberties. When your master
gets here I'll try and find out the things my mistress wants
to know about him by myself, if he seems worth the effort.
If you want to wait for him that room there is yours.

DORANT: Good heavens, here comes my master now!
(*Enter ARLECCHINO.*)

ARLECCHINO: Ah! There you are, Birmingham! My suitcase
and I, 'ave they been well received?

DORANT: It is hardly possible we should be other than well
received in a house such as this, sir.

ARLECCHINO: Dinestars said, Do Go Orn Up, we'll inform
your Farther In Lore and Waif that yoor 'ere.

SILVIA: You mean to say Mr Prowde and his daughter, sir, I'm
sure.

ARLECCHINO: Eh? Yah, Farther in Lore, Waif, same thing.
Get Engaged, Get Married, is all organised – Wedding? –
A Mere Detail, What?

SILVIA: A Detail which requires some consideration, one
would have thought.

ARLECCHINO: Yes, but once One has Thought Once About
One's Marriage One Tends Never To Think About It
Again Does One?

SILVIA: (*To DORANT.*) Apparently men of good family can be
rather in-bred where you come from, Birmingham.

ARLECCHINO: And what are the staff saying, miss?

SILVIA: Nothing, I was just saying that I'll ask Mr Prowde to
come down.

ARLECCHINO: Ah, yes, Farther In Lore.

SILVIA: He isn't, yet.

DORANT: She is right, sir – after all the marriage hasn't
actually taken place yet.

ARLECCHINO: But One Has Come Specifically to Ensure that
it Does.

DORANT: But you should still wait until it has –

ARLECCHINO: Good Heavens! Father in Law today, Father in
Law tomorrow, what's the difference?

SILVIA: In fact there's hardly any difference between being
married and not being married is there really, sir, so I'll
just run off and tell your father-in-law that you're here.

ARLECCHINO: Don't forget the Waif. And tell me something,
you pretty-little-thing-you…are you the…chambermaid…
in this Hestablishment?

SILVIA: If you say so, sir.

ARLECCHINO: Oh good, That makes me very happy. Will the
Famly Approve? Whaddyou think?

SILVIA: I think you're…terrifically amusing.

ARLECCHINO: Oh Good! I might take you up on that later…

SILVIA: And very becoming it is in you, sir, to be so modest
about it. Now you must excuse me, downstairs must have
forgotten to tell your father-in-law or I'm sure he'd be here
by now, I'll go myself.

ARLECCHINO: Do say One is so Looking Forward to meeting
him.

SILVIA: How very odd. Neither of these men know their
proper place.
(*Exit SILVIA to search for MR PROWDE.*)

SCENE 8

ARLECCHINO: Eh, sir, not a bad entrance, eh? The maid
   fancies me already.

DORANT: Lout.

ARLECCHINO: What? I entered like a real gent.

DORANT: You made me a solemn promise you would desist
   from your ridiculous manner of speech. I coached you
   exactly. I gave you strict instructions to take the situation
   seriously. Well, I see now I was a fool to trust you.

ARLECCHINO: I get much better in the next scene. I will do
   The Serious; and if that doesn't do the trick, I'll do The
   Upset – and if it is really necessary, I'll even do The Cry!

DORANT: I don't know where I am with this any more; the
   whole thing's giving me a headache. What the hell am I
   going to do?

ARLECCHINO: The daughter's no good then?

DORANT: Oh do shut up!

   (*Enter MR PROWDE and MAURICE.*)
   This is Mr Prowde.

SCENE 9

PROWDE: My dear sir, a thousand apologies for having kept
   you waiting – they've only just told me that you're here.

ARLECCHINO: My Dear Sir, a Thizand? Surely Nought; One
   Mistake, One Apology – but Anyway, Do 'elp yourself to
   as many of Main as you want.

PROWDE: I shall attempt to ensure that I have no further need
   of them.

ARLECCHINO: I am, Sir, At Your Service. No, I mean I am not
   Sir, at your service, I am NOT a servant, no, yes, master,
   servant etc, etc.

PROWDE: Anyway, I'm delighted to meet you – I've been so
   looking forward to it.

ARLECCHINO: Of Coarse One would have come Orn earlier
   with Birmingham here but when One has been Travelling
   One knows Wart a State One gets into and One simply felt
   uneasy Bite presenting Oneself before One had had Time
   to change into something a little more…Tastier.

MAURICE: The desired effect has been achieved.

PROWDE: Quite. My daughter's just dressing; she's been feeling a little unwell – while we're waiting for her to come down, may I offer you a little refreshment?

ARLECCHINO: Oh, One will drink with anybody.

(*There is a problem with the refreshments: LISETTE is still dressing; DORANT doesn't know what a butler really does, and SILVIA certainly isn't fetching ARLECCHINO a drink. So MR PROWDE rings the bell in vain... Anyway, eventually somehow the drinks get served.*)

PROWDE: Birmingham – my dear boy – do have a glass yourself.

ARLECCHINO: Used to drinking the Best you know this Fellow. Got Quite a taste for the Finer Things in Life.

PROWDE: Well I hope he'll feel free to indulge it.

(*The Four Men Have a Drink. LISETTE makes her Big Entrance dressed as SILVIA. The Men React. SILVIA, watching from the wings, sees 'herself'. MAURICE sings a song about Love.*)

Act Two

SCENE 1

(*Afternoon.*

SILVIA has met DORANT, LISETTE has met ARLECCHINO; the game has begun. How is it going?

MR PROWDE is alone on stage. Enter LISETTE.)

PROWDE: And what can I do for you, Lisette?

LISETTE: I have to see you for a minute.

PROWDE: What about?

LISETTE: I thought you ought to know how it's going so you're not in the dark and I won't be to blame.

PROWDE: This all sounds very serious.

LISETTE: Yes very serious. You gave Miss Silvia permission to get dressed up, well at the time I didn't think there was any harm in it either, and I was wrong wasn't I.

PROWDE: And what harm is there in it now?

LISETTE: Well Sir, far be it from me to blow my own trumpet but; it sounds improper I know but I have to tell you that if you don't take a firm hand this son-in-law you've organised isn't going to have anything left to give the Mistress your daughter on her wedding day, and I think she should tell him who she really is now, as a matter of some urgency; if she waits till tomorrow morning well then I shan't be held responsible.

PROWDE: And what makes you think he wouldn't still want her, after he knew who she really was? Aren't you rather underestimating her powers of attraction?

LISETTE: No Sir but you're not estimating mine enough. They're having their wicked way and I'm advising you not to let them get away with it.

(*MR PROWDE laughs.*)

PROWDE: Please accept my heartiest congratulations, Lisette.

LISETTE: Well there we are then, very amusing sir I'm sure, the joke's on me, but I'm sorry, it's you who's going to get sent the bill.

PROWDE: That really need not concern you, Lisette; you just carry on.

LISETTE: Alright I'll say it again. He isn't wasting any time. At lunch he said he liked me, at dinner he'll tell me he loves me and by tomorrow morning I expect he'll be offering me adoration on a permanent basis. It's all in the worst possible taste, a girl like me doesn't deserve it, you can say what you like, that doesn't mean it's not happening. You do see what I mean. By this time tomorrow I'll have been adored.

PROWDE: I don't see why you should find that a problem. If he loves you that much, I expect he'll marry you.

LISETTE: What! You'd stop it.

PROWDE: No, I wouldn't – I give you my word as a gentleman – if you can get him to go that far –

LISETTE: I'm warning you, sir. Up to this point I have done nothing to enhance my natural assets, I've just let them get on with it, and he's already hotting up. If I set to work, he'll boil over, and then that will be that.

PROWDE: Boil, poach, scramble and then marry him with my blessing – if you think you can.

LISETTE: I think I'm going to be a very rich girl.

PROWDE: Oh and by the way, has my daughter spoken to you at all? What does *she* make of her intended?

LISETTE: Well we hardly have a moment to talk about it really, seeing as how he never leaves me alone. But I should say, from the look of things, she's not best pleased. Put out. I'm just waiting for her to tell me to get rid of him.

PROWDE: Now that I forbid you to do. I am also avoiding talking to her – I have my own reasons for prolonging the proceedings – I want her to have plenty of time to make up her mind about her future husband. And how is the chauffeur behaving himself? Not entertaining any ideas about my daughter I hope?

LISETTE: He's a funny one. Comes on very grand with her I've noticed, fancies himself. Looks at her and sighs a lot.

PROWDE: And does she mind?

LISETTE: No…but she does blush.

PROWDE: Good – surely not; it takes more than a sighing chauffeur to embarrass her.

LISETTE: She's blushing.

PROWDE: With indignation, I expect.

LISETTE: Yes I expect that's it.

PROWDE: Anyway when you do get a chance to talk to her I want you to tell her that you suspect the chauffeur of trying to prejudice her against his master – and if she gets upset, don't let it concern you – that's my lookout.

SCENE 2

(*Enter ARLECCHINO.*)

PROWDE: I take it Mr Dorant here is looking for you.

ARLECCHINO: Ah, there you are, [you fabulous creature you]; I 'ave enquired after you all over. At Your Service, Dear Farther In Lore Practically Anyway.

PROWDE: At yours. Well, I'll leave you two alone together. I approve of you young people getting to know each other a bit before you get married.

ARLECCHINO: One would be Quite Happy to do the Two Jobs At Once.

PROWDE: Now let's not get too hasty. Good afternoon.

(*Exit MR PROWDE.*)

SCENE 3

ARLECCHINO: Madam, High Ham Hinstructed not to get too Hasty. High Ham 'Owever of the Hopinion that 'Aste is only Inappropriate in the Hold.

LISETTE: I can scarce believe Patience should be such a Trial, Sir, and think you play th'Impatient out of Gallantry merely – after all you have only just got here. A love so newly born as yours can scarcely be so Lusty an Infant.

ARLECCHINO: Ah, there you're wrong, oh wonder of the age – A love such as mine cannot idle in the cradle. The first time I saw you, he sprang into life. The second, he started to grow Up. [The third], he is a Big Boy… [Mother! Take care of your Child!]

LISETTE: Once he's big enough to go out to work I'm sure I can help you find him a suitable position. I should hate people to think that I lack maternal instincts.

ARLECCHINO: Perhaps until such time as he gets on the job you could offer him your lily-white hand to keep him amused.

LISETTE: There we are then, oh what a greedy little boy we are, I can see Mummy and Daddy aren't going to get a moment's peace unless you're kept happy.

ARLECCHINO: [Little darling baby's-rattle of my soul! You refresh those parts other beers cannot reach!]

LISETTE: That's enough, let's not be too greedy.

ARLECCHINO: [But I'm still thirsty etc etc.]

LISETTE: Now now, let's be reasonable.

ARLECCHINO: [Reason! Ohime! I have lost it. Your darling eyes have stolen it!]

LISETTE: But is't possible you should love me so much? I find it scarcely credible.

ARLECCHINO: Credible, incredible – let's not worry about that – I love you – madly! Why do I love you? – *Regardez dans votre miroir…*

LISETTE: I rather think *mon miroir* would only remind me of how unlikely the whole situation is.

ARLECCHINO: [Ah! What an adorable little darling!] Madam, Your Modesty is but Hypocrisy…

(*LISETTE and ARLECCHINO are just about to investigate the whole issue of Modesty and Hypocrisy when there is a knock on the door –*)

LISETTE: Someone's coming.

SCENE 4

(*Enter DORANT.*)

DORANT: Excuse me sir, could I see you for a moment.

ARLECCHINO: No! [Curse Him!] (*To LISETTE.*) Servants!! Nought a Moment's Peace!

LISETTE: Oh do see what he wants.

DORANT: Just one word, sir.

ARLECCHINO: Madam, if he attempts Two, the Third will be 'You Are', and the Fourth, 'Fired'. [Do excuse me.]

DORANT: Come over here, idiot. (*He hits him.*)

ARLECCHINO: [You said one word, not one smack –] (*To LISETTE.*) My Queen, do excuse me.

LISETTE: Oh by all means.

DORANT: Now just you stop all this at once or you'll give the game away; you're supposed to be being serious, sensitive and a little distressed; are you listening to me?

ARLECCHINO: [Yes yes I'm listening; don't you worry and now clear off.] (*DORANT is amazed by this far too idiomatic rendering of the line, so ARLECCHINO says it again in a different style in order to get him to go:*) Quite, Quite, Nothing to Worry About, That will be All.

(*Exit DORANT.*)

SCENE 5

ARLECCHINO: [Now, where was I...ah, yes...] Madam, Before we were so rudely interrupted... High was A Bite to say... Something, refained. But now...high fained my mained is come over all Common, on account of my love, which is so very extraordinary... And speaking of Love, do you think yours feels like sitting over here with mine?

LISETTE: Let us hope that one day it will.

ARLECCHINO: Will it be long?

LISETTE: What a very direct question; I'm almost embarrassed –

ARLECCHINO: [What do you expect: when a man is on fire, he has to call for the fire brigade!!]

LISETTE: Though of course were it socially acceptable for a woman in my position to speak frankly of what she really feels inside –

ARLECCHINO: [Please feel free to he absolutely frank –]

LISETTE: But sadly the modesty of my sex forbids it –

ARLECCHINO: [I had heard that modesty was going out of fashion these days –]

LISETTE: What are you asking me to do!

ARLECCHINO: [Tell me a little that you love me. Listen:] High Love You. [Repeat after me:] High Love You... [Princess; come on...] High Love You etc. etc.

LISETTE: Oh you insatiable beast! (*They play the repeating game together until finally LISETTE says:*) I love you!

ARLECCHINO: (*Climbing the walls.*) [Oh! I'm dying! I'm going crazy! I think I'm going to have to climb the walls!!] HUE LOVE ME!!!

LISETTE: I must confess myself a little alarmed by the sudden onset of this devotion. Don't you ever worry that one might love someone less once one gets to know them better?

ARLECCHINO: Ah! Madam –

LISETTE: You think I'm the perfect Lady, but, for instance, I might not be at all…

ARLECCHINO: [And you think I'm a perfect Gentleman.]

LISETTE: After all I am not the Mistress…of my own fate –

ARLECCHINO: [And I am not the Master –]

LISETTE: Although speaking for myself I am sure I should have been attracted to you whatever class of person you'd been –

ARLECCHINO: (*Who by this time is grovelling, beginning his build up to full prostration at the end of the scene.*) [Be attracted to me! Be attracted to me!]

LISETTE: May I flatter myself to think that you feel just the same way about me?

ARLECCHINO: Signora, if when I first saw you you had been the – [how do you say it] – the Maid! – you would still be *la mia principessa.*

LISETTE: Let's hope you'll always feel the same way about me.

ARLECCHINO: Let us do more than hope; let us swear –

LISETTE: – to love one another for ever, disregarding any minor violations of the agreed rules of socially acceptable behaviour which you may or may not find yourself inspired to commit on my behalf –

ARLECCHINO: *Sì.*

LISETTE: I couldn't agree more.

ARLECCHINO: [Your kindness overwhelms me and I prostrate myself before it.]

LISETTE: Oh no please. I can't possibly bear to look at you in that position. It was silly of me to have let you. Do get up.

(*There is of course a knock on the door.*)
There's somebody coming again.

SCENE 6

(*Enter SILVIA.*)

LISETTE: What do you want, Lisette?

SILVIA: I have to talk to you, madam.

ARLECCHINO: (*To LISETTE.*) [Wouldn't you know it!] (*To SILVIA.*) Sweetheart… (*He gives her a big tip.*) Fifteen minutes… (*SILVIA refuses to leave.*) Wear High Come Frorm, Maids Honely Come Hwen Their Corled.

SILVIA: Beggin' your pardon sir but I have to speak to Madam.

ARLECCHINO: [What a stubborn maid.] (*To LISETTE.*) [Queen of my life…get her off!] (*To SILVIA.*) That Will Be Hall! Listen, he told us to get to know each other before we got married, now can't you see we're busy.

LISETTE: Perhaps you could come back in a short while, Lisette.

SILVIA: Yes Ma'am, but –

ARLECCHINO: (*Losing his temper.*) [But! But! But excuse me for getting so angry!]

SILVIA: What a revolting man. I'm sorry Ma'am but the matter is rather pressing.

LISETTE: (*To ARLECCHINO.*) Would you excuse me?

ARLECCHINO: [Oh no, excuse me, I must be patient, I must just go for a little walk while she takes her time saying what she has to say.] One Simply Can't get The Staff These Days.

(*Exit ARLECCHINO.*)

SCENE 7

SILVIA: Well, I think it's utterly charming of you to have dismissed him so promptly and thus spared me the indignity of being in the same room at the same time as that *beast*.

LISETTE: 'Scuse me, madam, but I can't do two parts at once here; either I'm maiding or I'm mistressing.

SILVIA: Quite; and now that he is no longer with us you will, when I say that I must speak with you, kindly respond as a Maid. It must be quite clear to you that this man isn't at all suitable –

LISETTE: You haven't had time to examine him all over yet.

SILVIA: Examine him? Need one look twice in order to see how unsuitable he is? He's quite simply out of the question. Apparently my father doesn't share my repugnance; he's deliberately avoiding me. Since that is the case, I shall have to rely on you to extricate me from this delicate situation by discreetly suggesting to this gentleman that you are *not* inclined to accept his kind offer of marriage.

LISETTE: I couldn't do that, madam.

SILVIA: You couldn't. And why not?

LISETTE: Your father has forbidden me.

SILVIA: That doesn't sound like Father. Forbidding anything is usually quite outside his range.

LISETTE: Absolutely forbidden me.

SILVIA: Well perhaps you would be so kind as to inform him of my aversion and assure him that it's definite; when you have, he won't want to pursue this any further.

LISETTE: 'Scuse me for asking, madam, but what is it about this fiancé that's so revolting exactly?

SILVIA: I told you, I don't care for him. And I don't much care for your attitude either.

LISETTE: You just need the time to get to really know him, that's all.

SILVIA: I disliked him quite enough on superficial acquaintance not to want to spend any time getting to dislike him intimately.

LISETTE: His chauffeur, the one with the manners, he hasn't said anything to make you think like that about him?

SILVIA: The last thing we need in this situation is a chauffeur.

LISETTE: It's just I shouldn't trust him, too much of a way with his words.

SILVIA: Now please don't start with one of your thumbnail personality sketches, we can do without them. I have only allowed the chauffeur to engage me in the barest minimum

of conversation, but I must say I found the few words he
did exchange with me remarkably perceptive.

LISETTE: I think he looks just the sort who'd make unsuitable
remarks to show off how clever he was.

SILVIA: Well one is rather exposed to comment, dressed like
this. What exactly are you driving at? Where on earth
did you get the preposterous idea that this boy is the
reason why I loathe his master, when he has got nothing
to do with it. And yes, alright, I did make a fool of myself
listening to his stories but that is no reason to get him into
trouble with his employer or to make him out to be some
sort of double dealer or fraud.

LISETTE: Well madam, if we're going to adopt that tone in
his defence and if we're going to upset ourselves then I've
nothing more to say on the matter I'm sure.

SILVIA: If I'm going to adopt what tone in his defence? And
what about your tone? What are you trying to imply? Are
you hinting at something?

LISETTE: I was merely saying, madam, that I've never seen
you in such a state and I can't think what I've done to
be spoken to so sharply. And if the chauffeur didn't say
anything, well, that's alright then, there's no need for you
to get so worked up on his behalf, I believe you, there's
an end to the matter and far be it from me to take against
someone you were carrying a torch for I'm sure.

SILVIA: There you are you see that is exactly the sort of thing I
have to put up with, twisting and turning every word I say.
It makes me all so vexed, I could quite frankly cry.

LISETTE: Why's that then, madam? I hope you're not reading
double meanings into things.

SILVIA: Oh so now I'm reading double meanings. I'm getting
worked up on his behalf. I'm carrying a torch. Carrying
a torch dear God. Me, carry a torch. Have *all* the rules of
normal behaviour been suspended? What on earth do you
expect me to say, what am I to presume that you mean,
where do you think we are and just who exactly do you
think you're talking to?

LISETTE: I really couldn't say. It'll take me a while to recover
    my poise. How very surprising.
    (*Exit LISETTE.*)
SILVIA: She sometimes has a way of putting things that can
    make one feel quite…out of character. Thank you. You
    may go now. I find you quite intolerable. I should rather be
    on my own. I can manage.
    (*SILVIA alone.*
    Music.)

SCENE 8

Chase Number One

(*The rules:*
– DORANT must find SILVIA.
– SILVIA must be alone; SILVIA must avoid ARLECCHINO.
– LISETTE must get to work on ARLECCHINO.
– ARLECCHINO must find LISETTE.
– MR PROWDE must avoid SILVIA but at the same time keep an eye
on her.
– MAURICE must amuse himself.
During the chase, people rehearse fragments of text for their forthcoming
scenes. LISETTE quick-changes her way through four increasingly effective
frocks. The chase must climax with LISETTE and ARLECCHINO almost
managing to get together, but being prevented by SILVIA.
DORANT texts:)
1 Lisette, I – Lisette I want to – Lisette I have to, I really have
    to –
2 Lisette, notwithstanding the distance you feel there is
    between us – Lisette – notwithstanding the fact that you
    hold yourself so distant from me, that you keep yourself to
    yourself – that you are somehow –
3 Lisette, though you're keeping your distance yet I feel
    myself bound to talk to you, I find myself talking to you even
    when we're apart, even when you're not there I feel –
4 Lisette I know you're trying to avoid me but I have to talk
    to you.
(*SILVIA texts:*)

1 I am still shaking from that last scene. The sheer insolence with which the staff assume one shares their below-stairs attitudes. They drag one down to their level. I have tried to calm down but I'm sorry I can't. I daren't even think of some of the expressions she used or I'll set myself off again. After all, it's a chauffeur we're talking about. A chauffeur. Really!

2 A chauffeur. It's inconceivable. The mere suggestion is horrible and I shall dismiss it from my mind. And I shan't take it out on him.

3 Well it isn't his fault. After all, it's a chauffeur we're talking about. Really. The mere suggestion. I mean look at him, that is what I'm getting myself into such a state over. Well it's not his fault the poor boy and I mustn't take it out on him.

SCENE 9

DORANT: Lisette – I know you're trying to keep your distance but really, I must speak to you – I have a complaint to make.

SILVIA: Birmingham, don't let's be too familiar, please.

DORANT: If you like, I won't be.

SILVIA: I don't. But you are being.

DORANT: So are you then. You said 'Please'.

SILVIA: Words sometimes fail me.

DORANT: It seems a pity to waste what little time we have left in each other's company in formalities.

SILVIA: Oh, is your master leaving? Not that I'd mind if he was –

DORANT: Nor if I was. I was just finishing your line for you.

SILVIA: I am quite capable of finishing my own lines when I want to. You never entered my head.

DORANT: I can't get you out of mine.

SILVIA: Listen, Birmingham, and this is the last time I'll say this, stay, leave, come back, I really shouldn't mind which you do and I don't, I don't care one way or the other, I don't hate you, and I don't love you – and I won't ever love you, at least not unless I go completely mad. That's the way I feel, it would be quite unreasonable of me to feel any other way, and it's only fair I tell you as much.

DORANT: I am unimaginably unhappy. I rather think you may have ruined my life.

SILVIA: What on earth did he think was going on – oh the poor boy – Now get a hold of yourself. You're talking to me, I'm talking to you, and that's quite enough, in fact it's a little too much, believe you me, and if you were a little more experienced in these things – I mean – if you understood what was really going on – you'd understand that I'm just doing what's proper: you'd realise that I'm only acting out of the kindness of my heart, in fact if I saw another woman being this kind I'd tell her she was making a fool of herself; not that I feel a fool, because I know that what I'm doing is right. Now as I say I'm only telling you all this in order to be kind, and I must stop now, that sort of kindness is all very well in the heat of the moment but I'm not the sort of woman who can keep on reassuring herself of the innocence of her intentions all night and so really, in the end, the whole thing doesn't make any sense. So let's just stop all this shall we, just stop it, Birmingham. Please. After all, what's the point, it's a joke, so, I really think that's all there is to say.

DORANT: Lisette, do you have any idea of how much pain I'm in?

SILVIA: Now, you had something you wanted to say to me; you came in, and you said you had a complaint to make; well, about what?

(*DORANT goes out and attempts to replay the scene from the top. Enter DORANT.*)

DORANT: Lisette I know you're trying to keep your distance but really…really I must speak to you Lisette I have a complaint to make – oh it was nothing, nothing at all really. I just wanted to look at you and it seemed like a good excuse.

SILVIA: What can I say? I've tried being strict and it gets me nowhere.

(*DORANT tries again.*)

DORANT: Lisette I have to talk to you. I have a complaint to make. Your mistress has accused me of speaking disparagingly about my master to you.

SILVIA: Well she's imagining it, and if she accuses you again you should tell her as much straight out and then leave me to deal with her…

DORANT: Actually that wasn't it.

SILVIA: Well if that's all you had to say then I think that's the end of this scene.

(*SILVIA goes to exit, but:*)

DORANT: Please let me at least look at you.

SILVIA: Now that is a good reason for me to stay. I am to arouse passion in Birmingham. One day I am going to look back at all this and I am going to laugh.

DORANT: You're right, this is a complete farce, I don't know what I'm saying or what I want from you. Goodbye.

(*DORANT makes an exit, but:*)

SILVIA: Goodbye, yes, I'm sure that's for the best – but, speaking of goodbyes, there is just one thing I'd like to know. Your master and you are leaving, you said, was that bit serious?

DORANT: If I don't leave then I shall go mad.

SILVIA: That wasn't the answer I was hoping for.

DORANT: And my biggest mistake was not leaving the moment I met you.

SILVIA: I must remember to forget every single thing he says.

DORANT: If you only knew, Lisette, what an odd situation I'm in.

SILVIA: Not half so odd as mine, I assure you.

DORANT: What have I done wrong? It's not as if I've made myself attractive.

SILVIA: Oh no of course not.

DORANT: – and anyway what good would it do me to try and make you love me. Even if you were to fall in love –

SILVIA: From which fate Heaven preserve me. And if I did, you wouldn't even notice. I'd do it so well I wouldn't even know I'd done it myself. Really, the very idea.

DORANT: It is really true then, that you don't hate me, you
don't love me, and you won't ever love me?

SILVIA: There's no question.

DORANT: I have one. What makes me such an appalling
prospect?

SILVIA: Nothing; you're not the problem.

DORANT: Alright then. Say 'I won't ever love you' a hundred
times.

SILVIA: Oh I think once was enough. You have to try to
believe that I mean what I say.

DORANT: You're right. I have to. So, make my reckless
passion pointless; save me from it, tell me I'm a fool to fear
its consequences; you *don't* hate me, you *don't* love me, you
won't *ever* love me, go on, make it drown out the beating
of my frantic heart, because believe me, I am trying, but
I'm struggling, I'm struggling with myself, and I need your
help; I'm on my knees.

(*And he is. Enter MR PROWDE and MAURICE.*)

SCENE 10

SILVIA: Oh of course. I should have known we'd end up in
this position. God I feel a fool. It's my fault he's down
there. Do get up now Birmingham, please. Someone might
come in. I'll say whatever you want. What would you like
me to say? 'I don't hate you.' 'At all.' – Now do get up. 'I
would love you, if I could.' 'I don't not like you.' – Really
that's the best I can do.

DORANT: What? Lisette, if I wasn't who I am, if I was rich,
if I was a gentleman and if I loved you as much as I do
love you, do you think you wouldn't find me quite as
unattractive as you do?

SILVIA: Definitely –

DORANT: You wouldn't hate me. You'd put up with me.

SILVIA: Gladly. But you would have to get up.

DORANT: You said that as if you meant it and if you did then I
think I shall go mad.

SILVIA: I'm saying everything you want me to say and you're
still not getting up.

PROWDE: It seems a shame to interrupt you; you are doing
well my dears – bravo!

SILVIA: I did try and stop him getting on his knees, sir. But
then you can hardly be telling people what they can
do and what they can't do when you're in my position,
can you?

PROWDE: I should say both of you were in exactly the right
position – but we did want to have just a word, Lisette –
you can pick up where you left off after we've gone – is
that alright with you, Birmingham?

DORANT: I'll be going now, sir.

PROWDE: Do. Oh, and do try and speak of your master with a
little more discretion in future.

DORANT: Me, sir?

MAURICE: You sir, Birmingham; people do say that respect for
your employers is not your most outstanding feature.

DORANT: I don't know what they mean.

PROWDE: Thank you – thank you. You can explain yourself
on another occasion.

(*Exit DORANT.*)

SCENE 11

PROWDE: Well, Silvia, you don't seem able to look at us, you
look almost flustered –

SILVIA: Do I, Father? And what have I got to be flustered
about? I am feeling quite myself, thank God.

MAURICE: But there is definitely something going on, sister.

SILVIA: In your mind, possibly, brother dear, but in mine
there is nothing 'going on' except astonishment at your
suggestion that there might be.

PROWDE: Was that boy who's just left the one who has
inspired this violent antipathy towards his master?

SILVIA: Who – Dorant's man?

MAURICE: The dashing Birmingham.

SILVIA: If Birmingham is dashing it is news to me, and no, it
wasn't, because he never talks to me about his master.

PROWDE: Oh, I was told that it was he who'd been putting
 you off – and that was rather what I wanted to talk to you
 about –

SILVIA: There really wouldn't be any point, Father; the only
 person who has inspired my natural aversion for his master
 is his master.

MAURICE: How right you are, sister.

SILVIA: You make it all sound very mysterious.

MAURICE: Nerves, sister? You *are* in a state.

SILVIA: Because I am sick and I am tired of wearing this
 costume and if my father doesn't mind I would like to take
 it off now.

PROWDE: Not just yet, daughter. That's actually what I wanted
 to talk to you about. Since I was good enough to permit
 you your charade you will, if you don't mind, be good
 enough to suspend your judgement on Mr Dorant and
 to discover for yourself whether the opinion others have
 given you of him is correct.

SILVIA: You're really not listening to me are you? No one has
 given me any opinion.

MAURICE: Our over-talkative chauffeur hasn't made you feel a
 little squeamish about him?

SILVIA: What an objectionable way of putting it. 'Squeamish'.
 'Squeamish about him'. I seem suddenly to find myself
 surrounded on all sides by the most curious turns of
 phrase; deafened by the clash of infelicitous verb against
 inappropriate epithet. First I'm 'flustered', then something's
 'up', and now I'm being made 'squeamish' by someone
 'dashing'. All of which may make perfect sense to you but I
 don't understand a word.

MAURICE: I rather think it's you who are the curious turn.
 With whom, exactly, are you so angry; and why, exactly,
 are you being so defensive; and do you realise under what
 suspicions you are in danger of falling?

SILVIA: Never mind, brother. I'm sure it's simply bad luck
 that I find your vocabulary so grating this evening. Or is it
 that you're having one of your headaches; which suspicion
 exactly would you like me to fall under?

MAURICE: I must say you don't seem quite yourself to me either. I can only assume this is exactly the sort of outburst to which Lisette was referring. She simply enquired, she said, whether this chauffeur had spoken ill of his master to you and 'Madam,' as she put it, 'spoke up for him with such a passion that I am still all of a surprise' – we reprimanded her for this verbal infelicity – but then servants often don't quite know what they are saying.

SILVIA: How dare she. That girl is getting absolutely impossible. I was merely defending the boy against a patently unjust accusation.

MAURICE: An entirely natural impulse.

SILVIA: (*To MAURICE.*) Quite. Just because I am naturally fair-minded, because I don't like to see anybody getting hurt, because I wanted to save a servant from getting into his master's bad books, I'm described as having outbursts, losing my temper – which of course makes me completely surprising. Two seconds later one of the staff starts gossiping, naturally one gets annoyed, one tries to shut her up, one points out the merits of one's case – and she was the one who started it – my *case* – I suppose I had better prepare my defence now had I, acquire some alibis, make sure my evidence isn't open to misinterpretation. I stand accused. Well, of what – well do tell me somebody in case the charge is serious – or are we just joking – are we just making me a joke? I'm very upset.

PROWDE: Gently does it.

SILVIA: Gentleness has nothing to do with it. Surprises, consequences, why can't people just say what they mean. Someone accused the chauffeur, did they? Well they were wrong. You're wrong, Lisette's ridiculous, he's innocent, I've had enough. I don't know why we're still talking about it. Now I really am upset.

PROWDE: There's really no need to be so restrained, daughter. Perhaps you would like to speak your mind to me as well? Still, I'm sure we can do more than just talk about it. It's clear that the only suspect in the case is the chauffeur: Dorant will just have to send him away.

SILVIA: This ridiculous disguise. Don't let Lisette anywhere near me, I loathe her. Even more than I loathe this Dorant.

PROWDE: I'm sure you needn't see her unless you want to; but you ought to be delighted the boy's going, he's obviously fallen for you, which must be most annoying.

SILVIA: It doesn't bother me actually; he thinks I'm a maid and so that's how he talks to me – mind you, I don't let him just say what he likes, I keep a tight rein.

MAURICE: You're not quite as much the mistress of the situation as you say.

PROWDE: Didn't we just see him get down on his knees when you'd told him not to? And weren't you obliged to tell him that you didn't not like him before he'd get up off them? (*SILVIA chokes.*)

MAURICE: And furthermore, were you not, when he asked you whether you might one day love him, heard to tenderly utter the word 'gladly'? – without which word, one might conjecture, he might still be here.

SILVIA: Thank you for that learned summing-up, brother. But since I found the original incident unpleasant, I don't find the reprise very amusing either; and on that note, let's be serious for a moment. When is this comedy which seems to be being played at my expense, going to end?

PROWDE: I'm only asking that you don't decide to refuse him until you're in full possession of the facts. Give it just a little longer; you'll thank me for delaying the proceedings – I promise you.

MAURICE: I predict that you'll end up marrying this Dorant – and gladly… But Father, I would advocate clemency for the chauffeur.

SILVIA: Why? Personally I'll be glad to see him gone.

PROWDE: Let's leave it up to his master, shall we?
(*Exit MR PROWDE.*)

MAURICE: No hard feelings.
(*Music.*
SILVIA as if alone.
Exit MAURICE.)

SCENE 12

SILVIA: (*Seems to have a sudden palpitation.*) Oh dear, what
is the matter with my heart! I don't know if this is just
embarrassment or what – the whole situation seems so
fraught – I can't trust anyone. I don't like anyone. I don't
like myself.

(*Enter DORANT unseen.*)

DORANT: Ah! I was looking for you, Lisette.

SILVIA: Well I wasn't worth finding because I don't want to see
you.

(*She goes to exit.*)

DORANT: Don't go, Lisette, there's one final thing I have
to say to you – it's something important, about your
employers.

SILVIA: Go and say it to them then; every time I see you, you
upset me; now do leave me alone.

DORANT: I could say the same thing – but – do listen – really
– what I have to say will make everything different.

SILVIA: Alright then say it; I'm listening – I have been given
strict instructions that my patience with you must be
endless.

DORANT: Can you keep a secret?

SILVIA: I have never betrayed anyone.

DORANT: I wouldn't be confiding in you like this if I didn't
respect you so much.

SILVIA: I'm sure you wouldn't, but do try and respect me
without telling me about it, or I shall think this is another
one of your good excuses.

DORANT: It isn't, Lisette. You promised to keep this secret…
so, let's get to the point shall we… You've seen me at my
most wretched: I love you, I can't stop myself from saying
it –

SILVIA: Well I can stop myself from listening to it. Goodbye.

DORANT: Wait. This isn't Birmingham speaking to you any
more.

SILVIA: Oh really and who is it then?

DORANT: Lisette, now you'll see what sort of a mill my heart
has been through.

SILVIA: It's not your heart I'm talking to, it's you.

DORANT: Is anyone coming?

SILVIA: No.

DORANT: I've got to tell you, because of the mess things've got into; I'm too much of a decent sort really to let them carry on as they are.

SILVIA: Well?

DORANT: I think you should know the man who is with your mistress isn't who you think he is.

SILVIA: Who is he then?

DORANT: A chauffeur.

SILVIA: And.

DORANT: It's me who's Dorant.

SILVIA: (*Aside.*) Ah! Now I see how my heart works.

DORANT: I dressed up like this because I wanted to find out a bit about your mistress before getting engaged to her. It was all done with my father's consent – and now it's all turned into some dreadful dream. I hate the mistress who I was supposed to be marrying and I love the maid, who wasn't supposed to be anything except…the maid. What am I going to do? And I'm sorry to have to tell you this but your mistress has such poor taste in men that she's taken up with my chauffeur – to the point where she'd marry him if she could –

(*SILVIA stops him talking by kissing him. Then she turns to the audience:*)

SILVIA: I'm not going to tell him who I am.

INTERVAL

The action continues from exactly the point where it ended; SILVIA is kissing DORANT.

SILVIA: Well, what a novel situation you're in! Oh Sir, may I straightway offer my humble apologies if any remarks what have slipped into our conversations earlier have been at all irregular.

DORANT: Oh do shut up, Lisette, I can't stand it if you start apologising, it reminds me of all that keeps us apart, and I can't bear that.

SILVIA: You serious about me then? How much d'you love me?

DORANT: Well obviously someone like me can't marry someone like you – but enough not to want to have an affair with anybody else – I'd be happy staying single, knowing that you…'don't hate me'.

SILVIA: Since your heart has stooped so low as to notice me in my present condition, it would seem the least I can do is reciprocate. Which I would gladly do, were I not afraid of the possible consequences.

DORANT: Couldn't you just look like a lady, Lisette, without having to add speaking like one to your list of attractions?

SILVIA: Someone's coming! Don't do anything hasty about your chauffeur – there's no rush – we'll see each other again soon – I'm sure we'll be able to work something out –

DORANT: Whatever you say –

(*Exit DORANT.*)

SILVIA: Well, I wonder what I would have done if it hadn't been him.

SCENE 13

(*A small flurry of doors; ARLECCHINO, LISETTE, MAURICE.*)

MAURICE: I thought I'd better come and find you – we left you in such a state I was quite worried about you; I'm sure I can help, now listen –

SILVIA: There's some rather wonderful news. Everything's different.

MAURICE: What is?

SILVIA: It isn't Birmingham at all, it's Dorant.

MAURICE: What are you talking about?

SILVIA: About him, I just found out, he's gone now, he told me so himself.

MAURICE: Who did?

SILVIA: Didn't you hear what I said?

MAURICE: Yes but I'm blowed if I understood it.

SILVIA: Right, let's go; we must find Father, he really ought to know. I'll need your help too – I've just had an idea; pretend to be in love with me – I mean you've already hinted that you are, as a joke – but above all, don't give the game away.

MAURICE: How can I when I don't know what we're playing at?

SILVIA: So, brother dear, off we go; there's not a moment to lose. Nothing like this has happened to anybody ever. (*Exit SILVIA.*)

MAURICE: I do hope no one's going to become hysterical.
MAURICE sings a song about Love.

Chase Number Two

(*The rules:*

– MAURICE and MR PROWDE have to keep a much closer eye on things because they are moving that much faster.

– ARLECCHINO and LISETTE are getting pretty desperate.

– SILVIA is looking for her father.

– DORANT is nearly suicidal, and must avoid everyone but especially LISETTE.

*MAURICE, having finished his song, announces, 'The Same, After Dinner'.
Exit MAURICE.*)

Act Three

SCENE 1

ARLECCHINO: Ah! Monsieur, Sir, [Sir my most highly
    respected master I beg of you, I implore you etc etc...]

DORANT: Yes!!

ARLECCHINO: 'Pity a poor man, sir, don't snatch away 'is only
    chance of 'appiness just when it's within 'is grasp!'

DORANT: That's enough, d'you think I can't tell when you're
    trying to make a fool out of me? You deserve a bloody
    good hiding.

ARLECCHINO: I do, I do, you're right, who am I to refuse
    what I have deserved, would you like me to go and get the
    stick? And when I have had it, the bloody good, can I go
    and deserve it some more?

DORANT: I've had enough of your cheek.

ARLECCHINO: [I may be a] cheek; [but I am also going to be a
    rich] cheek.

DORANT: It's sad really. Idiot!

ARLECCHINO: [That's okay, if you are a] cheek [then you
    don't mind being called an] idiot. [But remember, sir;] rich
    people marry idiots.

DORANT: Don't be so insolent – now, let me get this right;
    you want me to be party to the deception of a respectable
    household, and to allow you to marry the daughter of that
    household while pretending to be me? Listen; if you even
    mention this gross impertinence again, no sooner shall I
    have informed our host who you really are than I shall give
    you your notice.

ARLECCHINO: *Aspetto. La Madame*, [she loves me. She adores
    me.] *Si* – if I say to her, '*io sono – le chauffeur*'; and, she says,
    '[That is not a problem,] High Still Love Hue.' – Well? –
    (*ARLECCHINO plays or sings 'Here Comes the Bride'.*)

DORANT: If she finds out who you really are then I don't think
    I shall really care what happens.

ARLECCHINO: [Good!] I shall [immediately] disabuse this
    [generous young person] as to the significance of my usual
    accoutrements. I trust that a few brass buttons will not

suffice to come between us, and that Love will see fit to usher me into The Drawing Room, even though Life has consigned me to The Garage.

(*Exit ARLECCHINO.*)

SCENE 2

DORANT: Everything that happens here – especially everything that's happening to me – is quite…unrealistic. I must see Lisette, and find out if she has had any joy trying to explain to her mistress and getting me out of this mess. If I could just catch her on her own –

Chase Number Three

(*The rules:*

– DORANT is looking for SILVIA but finds LISETTE.

– SILVIA is looking for her father – still rehearsing her text: 'If only you knew how much more all of this will make us love each other after we're married, if only you knew how grateful I'll be, how much I'll etc etc.'

– ARLECCHINO is looking for LISETTE.

– LISETTE is presumably going crazy.

– MR PROWDE sends MAURICE on to catch DORANT before he can get to SILVIA.)

MAURICE: Just a moment, Birmingham; could I have a brief word?

DORANT: What can I do for you, sir?

MAURICE: Have you been making suggestions to our Lisette?

DORANT: When one meets someone truly loveable it is hard not to talk like a lover.

MAURICE: And how does she take your speeches?

DORANT: Very lightly, sir.

MAURICE: You are amusing; are you…misleading her?

DORANT: No, I'm not; and if I were, would it concern you? Supposing that Lisette did have a penchant for me –

MAURICE: A 'penchant' for you – where did you pick that one up? Coming from a lad like you your vocabulary shows quite remarkable refinement.

DORANT: Sir, I shouldn't know how to talk any other way.

MAURICE: I imagine it is with just such flights of pretension that you have been assaulting our Lisette. Almost like a gentleman.

DORANT: I assure you, sir, I am not pretending to be anybody; but I am sure you didn't detain me simply in order to subject me to ridicule and that you do have something else you wanted to say to me? We were talking about Lisette: about my intentions towards her and why that should be any concern of yours –

MAURICE: Good heavens! I detect a certain touch of jealousy in the delivery of that line. Do calm down. Thank you. Now, you were telling me…supposing that Lisette had a penchant for you…and?

DORANT: And why should you be told if she did, sir.

MAURICE: Ah yes. That was it. Because…despite the musical comedy tone which I have heretofore affected, I should become quite melodramatic were she to love you; because – and I really don't want to discuss this – I forbid you any further intimate conversations with her; *not* because I'm afraid that she might actually fall for you, you understand – she seems to me to be above that sort of thing – but simply because I personally dislike having someone called Birmingham as a rival.

DORANT: I know just how you feel – because Birmingham, being your real, typical Birmingham sort, doesn't much like having you as his either.

MAURICE: He must be patient.

DORANT: Yes, he must. Do you love her a lot, sir?

MAURICE: Enough to make her a serious proposal once I have successfully concluded certain rather delicate negotiations. If you see what I mean.

DORANT: I rather think I do. In which case, of course, she must love you.

MAURICE: What do you think? Aren't I worth loving?

DORANT: You're not by any chance fishing for compliments from an acknowledged rival, are you?

MAURICE: A sensible riposte and one I shall forgive; but – and it's too mortifying really – I can't honestly say that she does

love me – and I'm not telling you this because I have to, as
I'm sure you are aware – I just happen to think one should
be frank in this sort of situation.

DORANT: You amaze me, sir; Lisette is not aware of your
plans for her?

MAURICE: Lisette is fully aware of all the good I could do her,
and yet appears not to be…susceptible – however I have
high hopes that she'll soon be…sensible, and be mine.
Thank you, that will be all – please don't make a scene.
The fact that she doesn't really want me despite all I've got
to give her will have to be sufficient consolation for the fact
that you've got to let me take her even though you don't
really want to… I hardly think that uniform's going to tip
the balance in your favour, and let's face it, you're hardly
equipped for fighting – someone like me.

SCENE 3

(*Enter SILVIA.*)

MAURICE: Ah, Lisette, there you are.

SILVIA: And what can I do for you sir, oh you look a bit upset
to me.

MAURICE: Oh it's nothing, I've just been having a word with
Birmingham here.

SILVIA: He looks a bit upset too – have you been telling him
off?

DORANT: The master has been telling me how much he loves
you, Lisette.

SILVIA: Well that's not my fault is it?

DORANT: And telling me not to love you.

SILVIA: Well he'd better tell me not to be so attractive then,
hadn't he?

MAURICE: I can't prevent him loving you, Lisette darling, but
I do rather mind him saying it to you.

SILVIA: Oh he doesn't say it anymore: he just repeats it.

MAURICE: Well he will at least avoid repeating it while I'm in
the room. You may go, Birmingham.

DORANT: I'm waiting for her to tell me to.

MAURICE: I'm sorry?

SILVIA: He said he's waiting; you'll have to wait, too.

DORANT: Do you like The Master?

SILVIA: Do I love him, you mean? Well let's just say I don't think it's going to be worth anyone's while telling me not to.

DORANT: You aren't playing with me?

MAURICE: You may go now. Apparently this isn't one of my more convincing roles. Excuse me, but to whom am I talking?

DORANT: You're talking to Birmingham.

MAURICE: Well would he mind leaving?

DORANT: This hurts.

SILVIA: Oh that's enough now or he's going to get angry.

DORANT: (*Aside to SILVIA.*) Perhaps you don't want anything better.

MAURICE: That'll do, thank you.

DORANT: You never said anything about loving someone else, Lisette.

(*Exit DORANT.*)

SCENE 4

SILVIA: I think not loving a man like that would smack rather of ingratitude, don't you?

(*MAURICE laughs; music. Enter MR PROWDE.*)

PROWDE: And what have you got to laugh about, Maurice?

MAURICE: Dorant has just made a splendidly angry exit because I (*CHORD.*) forced him (*CHORD.*) to leave (*CHORD.*) Lisette.

SILVIA: What on earth had you been saying to him in your little *tête-à-tête.*

MAURICE: I have never seen a grown man so intrigued or so distressed.

PROWDE: I am not at all sorry to see the boy hoist with his own petard – and after all it's not as if he's had too hard a time of it up till now – you could hardly have been more entertaining if you had tried, daughter – but now, I agree – I think we've gone far enough.

MAURICE: But how far exactly have we gone, sister?

SILVIA: Oh! I rather think I'm going to be happy.

MAURICE: 'Oh!' – *feel* the sweet certainty with which that syllable *was* inflected.

PROWDE: Daughter, are you anticipating that the boy will go so far as to get down on his knees and propose while he still thinks you're the maid?

SILVIA: Yes, Father dear, I am anticipating.

MAURICE: I love it when you act. 'Father Dear.' Now we have given our Shrew I suppose we're going to be all sweetness and light.

SILVIA: You don't miss a word.

MAURICE: 'Ah-ha! Now I take my revenge!' You pulled me up so short over my turns of phrase: it seems only fair I should now have a little fun with yours. Rest assured you're quite as amusing ecstatic as you were anxious.

PROWDE: At least you've got me on your side; you go ahead and do whatever you see *fit*.

SILVIA: Oh if you knew how grateful I'll be. Dorant and I, we were made for one another. He'll have to marry me – if you only knew how much I'll be in his debt too, after everything he's going through for me – and how much I'll cherish the memory of all the ridiculous things he's said – and if you knew how much more all of this is going to make us love each other after we're married – he won't ever be able to remember how we met without loving me, and I won't be able to think about it without loving him. You've made us happy for life by letting me do this; our marriage won't be like other people's. It won't be like other people's. It won't be like other people's; it'll be an adventure, even talking about it makes me want to cry; and to think it all happened by chance! I'm so lucky. I am so happy. I am so…

MAURICE: …good at making long speeches. Funny how eloquent cheap emotions can be.

PROWDE: Of course we all find romantic fiction charming – especially when it comes true. Do you think you can actually make it happen?

SILVIA: It already has. He's quite overcome. I await my
captive.

MAURICE: The cage may be a little more gilded than the
bird expects, but I'm not sure he's at all happy with the
prospect of captivity, I find his plight rather moving.

SILVIA: The more it costs him to make up his mind the more
he's worth to me. He thinks he can only have me at the
expense of disobeying his father. He thinks he is betraying
both The Family and The Family Fortune. Hardly
inconsiderable obstacles. I shall delight in triumphing
over them. But I want to snatch my victory from the jaws
of opposition, not to have him hand it to me on a plate. I
want a battle royal between Reason and Passion.

MAURICE: And you want Reason to be lost.

PROWDE: What you actually want is for him to suffer the
full imaginary consequences of the step he will think he
is making. Strange how Self-Respect can lead one to a
monstrous disregard for others.

MAURICE: Oh women are like that: they understand that
Vanity and Self-Respect are the same thing.

(*A glorious scream from LISETTE; ARLECCHINO has finally not
been able to wait any longer.*)

SCENE 5

PROWDE: Ah, that must be Lisette. I wonder what she wants.
(*Enter LISETTE in violent déshabille. ARLECCHINO can be heard
warming up for his big scene.*)

LISETTE: Sir, you did say you were leaving him up to me, that
you were placing him entirely in my hands; well I have
taken you at your word. I've gone to work on him as if I
was on one of my own jobs and, as you are about to see, a
very good job has been done too. He's all nice and ready.
What d'you want me to do with him now? Is Madam going
to hand him over?

PROWDE: Well, daughter, speak now or for ever hold your
peace.

SILVIA: You can have him, Lisette; I hereby renounce any
prior claim I may have in the matter, and hereby swear

that I have no interest in any hearts except those I have, as you put it, got nice and ready all by myself.

LISETTE: You really want me to marry him. Sir really wants me to marry him too.

PROWDE: Yes; if he'll have you. What does he see in you?

MAURICE: I can see no just impediment –

LISETTE: Neither can I and thank you all very much –

(*LISETTE goes to exit and get to work, but:*)

PROWDE: Oh – just one minor proviso; so that we're not held responsible for any possible consequences – you'll have to give him just a hint as to who you really are.

LISETTE: If I give him a hint, he'll get it.

PROWDE: I'm sure he's nice and ready enough to be able to stand the shock. He doesn't seem the oversensitive type.

(*ARLECCHINO and his preparations for the scene cannot be ignored any longer.*)

LISETTE: That's him looking for me. Everybody off please; this is my big scene.

PROWDE: Quite. Shall we go?

SILVIA: Gladly.

MAURICE: Do let's.

(*They exit. LISETTE arranges herself and the lighting. She may possibly sneak MAURICE back on to provide romantic accompaniment; if so, she also dismisses him later.*)

SCENE 6

(*Enter ARLECCHINO.*)

ARLECCHINO: Darling, at last. Now that I've found you I'll never let you go – every moment away from you has been sheer hell – I was afraid perhaps you didn't want to see me again.

LISETTE: Yes, I must say, it was something like that.

ARLECCHINO: Darling, don't you know that I'd die? You don't want me to die, do you?

LISETTE: No I don't, darling, you have no idea how much you're worth to me –

ARLECCHINO: [Ah! Hearing you say that makes me feel so much better.]

LISETTE: And you mustn't ever doubt the depth of my feelings for you –

ARLECCHINO: [I would like to kiss every one of those words and pluck them from your lips with mine.]

LISETTE: But you were being so very pressing on the subject of our marriage, and my – father had not yet given me permission to give you my answer; however I have just spoken to him and he has told me that I can tell you that you can ask him for my hand any time you want.

ARLECCHINO: Just before I ask him for it – let me ask you for it – (*He produces a script which he has prepared earlier.*) 'I wish to tender unto it my heartfelt thanks for its graciousness in permitting itself to be joined in union with mine which is not in the same league at all.'

LISETTE: You may borrow my hand sir, on one condition; that you never return it.

ARLECCHINO: [Dear little chunky juicy hand-baby], I am lucky to get hold of it under any circumstances whatsoever. 'The honour you do me is great. The only problem here is the honour I'm doing you.'

LISETTE: You do me much more than I deserve.

ARLECCHINO: Ah. No. No. [No; *you* do *me* more than *I* deserve.]

LISETTE: To me your love is like a gift from Heaven.

ARLECCHINO: Oh it's nothing really.

LISETTE: But I really don't deserve it.

ARLECCHINO: Wait till you see it in the daylight.

LISETTE: You have no idea how embarrassing I find your modesty.

ARLECCHINO: You have no idea how modest I really am.

LISETTE: No, really, sir, must I spell it out, I am the one who is being honoured.

ARLECCHINO: [Ahi! I don't know where to put myself.]

LISETTE: Yes, believe me, sir, I know my place.

ARLECCHINO: I know mine, too. And the people I know there, they aren't up to much, and you won't be either. When you know. Them. But that's the funny thing about getting to know me, you never know what's at the bottom of the bag.

LISETTE: (*Aside.*) I always think there's something not quite right about men who apologise, don't you? What are you actually trying to say?

ARLECCHINO: The Cat's in the Bag. Waiting to be let out.

LISETTE: Yes. And. You've got me worried now. Are you trying to say that you're not –
(*ARLECCHINO lets the cat out of the bag.*)
I think we'd better have a little talk.

ARLECCHINO: *Aspetto!* (*In order to try and explain, he goes back to a earlier scene and sets it up again:*) Madam; do you remember: The first time I saw you our Love was born, the second time –

LISETTE: – the second time he started to grow up and now he's Big Boy, yes yes.

ARLECCHINO: Okay; now; is he Healthy? *Robusto?* How does he feel about working for a living? Does he like little rooms? Garages, for instance.

LISETTE: I don't think I can stand very much more of this. Who are you?

ARLECCHINO: *Io sono*…have you ever seen a fake five-pound note? A fake ten-pound note? *Io sono*… I am… I am a bit like a fake five-pound note –

LISETTE: Go on. What's your name.

ARLECCHINO: (*Aside.*) My name? If I say I'm Arlecchino, will she want to marry-me-no.

LISETTE: Well?

ARLECCHINO: [Madam, this isn't easy, alright?] Do you like gentlemen?

LISETTE: What sort of gentlemen?

ARLECCHINO: Gentlemen's gentlemen.

LISETTE: This isn't Mr Dorant I'm talking to is it?

ARLECCHINO: He's my guv'nor.

LISETTE: You bastard. You-mean-he – no!

ARLECCHINO: (*Aside.*) [Well at least it rhymed]

LISETTE: Ape!
(*LISETTE beats up ARLECCHINO.*)

ARLECCHINO: (*Apart.*) [Not bad the gymnastics, eh?]

LISETTE: And here's me spending the entire evening trying to impress *him* and wearing myself out feeling inferior to a showman's bleeding monkey.

ARLECCHINO: I'm sorry. But if being Loved is as good as being Posh, I can do it just as well as he does.

LISETTE: You've got to laugh really haven't you, him and his Posh, 'cause if you didn't laugh – never mind, eh? I'm sure I'm Posh enough to handle the situation. At least I'm sure I'm quite Posh enough for you.

ARLECCHINO: [Really?]

LISETTE: Really. So what if I've been made a fool – (*She takes his hand as if to make up.*) – A Gentleman's Gentleman deserves a Lady's Maid.

ARLECCHINO: A Lady's Maid?

LISETTE: She's my guv'nor. Or whatever you say when it's a woman who's the guv'nor.

ARLECCHINO: [Minx!]

LISETTE: Go on, feel free.

ARLECCHINO: And there's me spending the entire evening going all ashamed of my having no money.

LISETTE: Now let's talk business. D'you love me?

ARLECCHINO: [God!] *Si. Oui.* Yes. What I call you has changed but what I see has not changed. Anyway –

LISETTE: – anyway we did swear to love one another for ever disregarding any minor violations of the agreed rules of socially acceptable behaviour which we might find ourselves inspired to commit. So, not too much harm done is there – pretend nothing's happened. I don't want anyone laughing at us. (*Checks through the keyhole to see that no one has seen anything.*) It's your guv'nor – he's coming in here – (*Enter DORANT.*) Looks to me like he still hasn't worked out what's going on with my mistress; don't tell him anything – we'll leave things just the way they are – I am, sir, your humble servant.

ARLECCHINO: Madam; I'm one too.

(*Exit LISETTE.*)

SCENE 7

DORANT: Have you told her who you are yet?

ARLECCHINO: [Oh God yes. Poor child!] I said to her, '[I am called] Arlecchino, I am the Chauffeur'; 'Oh really dear boy,' she said, 'everyone has to have a name, everyone has to have a uniform. So, yours is not a suit – well, it suits you.'

DORANT: This is another one of your ridiculous stories.

ARLECCHINO: So I'm going to marry her.

DORANT: What! You proposed? She's accepted?

ARLECCHINO: [Oh yes of course she'd have to be mentally ill to do that.]

DORANT: You're making this up; she doesn't know who you are.

ARLECCHINO: You want to make a bet I marry her with my boots on? You make me angry – with my overalls on, okay? I would like you to know that when I love somebody it does not break easy, and that I don't need your suit for me to do it, and I have my clothes back now thank you.

DORANT: You're having me on – it's inconceivable…and I can see it's high time I had a word with Mr Prowde.

ARLECCHINO: [Who?] Oh, Farther in Lore. Splendid Old Chap. Got him right on board. Lovely Old Boy. Absolutely your first-class old boy. You were saying?

DORANT: You're incredible, you know that? Have you seen Lisette?

ARLECCHINO: Lisette? No. Possible she did pass before my eyes, but a real gentleman doesn't really notice – the Maid. I leave that sort of thing up to you.

DORANT: And you're insane. Now get out.

ARLECCHINO: Your manners leave a little to he desired my boy. But you'll find that comes with experience. (*Exit ARLECCHINO. Enter ARLECCHINO.*) When I am married, [we will he equal], you and me.
(*Enter SILVIA.*)

[Oh, here is your maid.] Good Evening Lisette. May I recommend the Birmingham. The boy's not without his redeeming features.

(*Exit ARLECCHINO.*)

SCENE 8

DORANT: Well you can understand why people love her… Damn Maurice for getting there first.

SILVIA: Where have you been, sir? Ever since that scene with Master Maurice I've been hunting for you all over the place to tell you what I've been telling Mr Prowde.

DORANT: How odd. I haven't been hiding myself. And what have you been telling him?

SILVIA: Well I can understand him being so cold, he – I told him, straight out I told him what I thought about this chauffeur and I said clearly the man's got no conscience and isn't at all suitable, I pointed out in no uncertain terms the very least he can do is postpone the wedding but no he wasn't having any of it. And just between you and me there's talk of it being time to book the church, so you'll have to give the game up now, won't you?

DORANT: I intend to. I'll leave a note explaining the situation to Mr Prowde and then slip off incognito.

SILVIA: Slip off. That wasn't the idea at all.

DORANT: I think that would be best, don't you?

SILVIA: But – not particularly.

DORANT: I can't think what else to do in this situation, except actually tell him myself of course, and I can't see me doing that. Besides, there are other reasons why I must leave; I really can't go on with this any longer.

SILVIA: Since I've no idea what these reasons of yours are I can't really sympathise and I can't really try and talk you out of them, can I? – and it's hardly my place to ask you to tell me what they are.

DORANT: It should be quite easy for you to suspect what they are, Lisette.

SILVIA: Well it had occurred to me that possibly you had taken a dislike to the master's daughter.

DORANT: Is that all that has occurred to you?

SILVIA: Well of course there are certain other things I might imagine – but then, I'm no fool, and I'm not vain enough to dwell on things like that.

DORANT: And not brave enough to talk about them – still, I don't expect anything you'd have to say would be anything I'd want to hear. Goodbye, Lisette.

SILVIA: I can see I'm going to have to spell it out, you really don't understand do you?

DORANT: Oh but I do. Perfectly. And making things clearer wouldn't make them any easier, so please, remain incomprehensible until after I've gone.

SILVIA: You're not actually going to go are you?

DORANT: You seem very afraid that I might change my mind.

SILVIA: How very sweet of you to be so perceptive.

DORANT: How very frank of you to say so.

(*DORANT makes his exit. During his exit:*)

SILVIA: If he leaves the room, how can I love him, I shan't hove him, I shan't ever marry him… Oh look he's stopping. He's thinking about it, he's looking to see if I'm turning my head – and I – and I don't know what to do to make him come back, I… Wouldn't it be funny if he did go, after I've gone to all this trouble. Well I suppose that's it then. He's gone. I don't have as much hold over him as I thought. God that brother of mine's useless, he went about it completely the wrong way. People who don't care about anything always ruin everything. And I was doing so well. Not much of an ending is it? Perhaps he'll come back on. I really do think he's coming back now – (*But he isn't.*)

(*She goes to exit; at which moment of course DORANT comes back on.*)

– I take it all back of course I love him – I'll pretend to leave – he'll have to stop me – it's always best when the reconciliation is a bit more difficult for the man –

DORANT: Stay – please – there's something I have to say to you.

SILVIA: To me, sir?

DORANT: I'm finding it very hard to leave without having
made you see that it's not my fault.

SILVIA: Oh, sir, you don't have to explain yourself to me. It's
not hard at all; I'm only the maid, as you've made me only
too well aware.

DORANT: I have? And who do you see having to put up with
everything and not saying a word – me – I don't see you've
any reason to find your position in all this particularly
difficult.

SILVIA: There's a really good answer to that. It's just that I
can't bring myself to say it.

DORANT: No, please, let's have it, I'd like nothing better
than to be told I've got this all wrong. Oh, but what am I
saying? Maurice loves you.

SILVIA: That's right.

DORANT: And you're quite happy that he loves you – as one
can see from the extreme vigour with which you sought
to prevent me from leaving – in which case of course you
couldn't possibly love me.

SILVIA: I'm happy. Who told you that? And I couldn't possibly
love you. How would you know? You're very sure about
everything.

DORANT: Listen, Lisette, for God's sake, please, tell me what's
going on. Please.

SILVIA: What can you tell a man when he's leaving you?

DORANT: I won't leave, ever.

SILVIA: OH STOP IT. Listen, if you love me, stop asking me
all these questions. You're scared I might have nothing to
say – and then you love it when I don't say anything – and
anyway what have my feelings got to do with you?

DORANT: What have they got to do with me? Lisette, you
can't still seriously doubt that I'm mad about you.

SILVIA: No I can't. You say it to me so very often that I'm
obliged to believe it, so why must you keep on trying to
persuade me of the fact and what do you want me to do
about it. Sir. Now I am going to be frank with you. You
love me; but your falling in love really isn't anything very
serious. Should you ever want to fall out of it again you'll

find Life makes that relatively easy for the likes of you. The distance between you and me; all the attractive women you're going to meet; how keen they're going to be on your being keen on them, all the distractions available to a young gent like you…all that'll get you out of what you're trying so hard to talk me into. I expect that when you leave here you'll have a good laugh about it all – and that'll be alright for you. But I, Sir, if I ever look back, as I'm rather afraid I shall, if I let myself succumb, what am I going to have to protect me against what you will have done to me? Who's going to compensate me if you've ruined me? Who's my heart going to get in as a replacement? You do realise that if I love you then all the things that matter most to me aren't going to matter any more. So you just stop for a bit and think about the state I'll be in. And be kind to me, sir. Conceal your love. And as for me – well, I should think twice about telling you I loved you in the state you're in – if I were to reveal my feelings that might really drive you mad, and anyway, as you can see, I'm concealing them from you.

DORANT: Oh darling Lisette. The way you talk, the things you say – go right through me. I adore you. I respect you. And what class I am, what Family I'm from, how much Money I have or won't have – well you make all that seem inconsequential. I'd be a fool to let my Pride hold out against you any longer. I offer you my hand, and believe me, my heart's in it.

SILVIA: Oh of course I couldn't really refuse an offer from a gent like you could I? And I can hardly conceal how happy I am to have been made it, can I? And do you really think this will last?

DORANT: You do love me?

SILVIA: No. No. And if you ask me just one more time that will be it.

DORANT: You can't scare me away.

SILVIA: What about Maurice? Aren't you bothered about him?

DORANT: No Lisette, Maurice doesn't bother me; you don't love him; you can't fool me any more. You care. You care

about me. I know you do, otherwise I wouldn't be feeling
what I am feeling, and nothing you can say can take that
away from me.

SILVIA: Oh I shan't try to, you can keep your feeling. And
now what are you going to do?

(*DORANT kneels.*)

DORANT: Be mine.

SILVIA: Oh so you're going to marry me, and never mind
Society and never mind your Father and never mind the
Money.

DORANT: My father will understand as soon as he sees you;
I'm sure my money will be enough for the two of us, and
who you are matters more than what society you keep, so
please don't argue with me any more, because I won't ever
change my mind.

SILVIA: He won't ever change. Do you have any idea how
charming I find you, Dorant?

DORANT: Don't lock your heart up any longer. Let it say what
it wants to say.

SILVIA: Alright then. This is finally it. You – you won't ever
change.

DORANT: No. No Lisette, I won't.

SILVIA: This is Love.

(*The rest of THE COMPANY enter, in evening dress, applauding,
with champagne.*)

SCENE 9

SILVIA: Ah, Father. You always said I should belong to
Mr Dorant. Well do come in, come in and watch your
daughter obey you with the very greatest of pleasure.

DORANT: What is this? You're her father?

SILVIA: Yes. You see we both had the same idea of getting to
know each other. And after that – well, what else can I
tell you? – you obviously love me, there was never really
any doubt about that – and if you are in any doubt about
my feelings – well I think you can judge how I feel about
you from the great lengths I have gone to get you where I
wanted you.

PROWDE: Do you recognise this letter? That was how I knew about your disguise – though she only knew because you told her.

DORANT: I can't tell you how happy I am. But I will just say that what makes me happiest is having had the chance to prove myself.

MAURICE: I trust Dorant will forgive me for making life so difficult for Birmingham?

DORANT: No he won't forgive you for it. He thanks you for it.
(*SILVIA takes off her apron.*)

EPILOGUE WITH MUSIC

(*The SERVANTS clear up now the MASTERS and MISTRESSES have finished their game. The house is dark and quiet, except for the piano.*)

ARLECCHINO: [Cheer up, missus.] You didn't get the money – you still got me.

LISETTE: Oh thanks a lot. That's very nice – for you.

ARLECCHINO: [That's true.] Before we found out who we really were you had lots of money and no class. Now you got no money. But you got plenty of class. You fancy a dance then?
(*The End.*)